The Front Line Guide to
BUILDING HIGH
PERFORMANCE TEAMS

Woodrow H. Sears

HRD Press, Inc. • Amherst • Massachusetts

Published by:

HRD Press, Inc.
22 Amherst Road
Amherst, MA 01002
800-822-2801 (U.S. and Canada)
413-253-3488
413-253-3490 (fax)
www.hrdpress.com

ISBN 0-87425-939-8

Production services by Jean Miller
Editorial services by Suzanne Bay
Cover design by Eileen Klockars

Table of Contents

Preface

This book was written to achieve two purposes: First, I wanted to present the concept of "team building" as an identifiable, observable, and replicable set of attributes that can be used by managers to shape any group of workers into a high performance team. Teams, team work, and team building have become such common topics in the literature on management that the concepts themselves seem to have lost their meaning.

The large task of this small book, then, is to reestablish the significance of team building as an intentional application of managerial strategies in order to increase the performance potential of any group of people (employees, volunteers) so they can accomplish specific tasks. Along the way, I hope to point out some team-building practices that I believe are inappropriate (and thus diminish the value of the concept) and will present some criteria for determining when team building is appropriate.

My second purpose for writing the book is to familiarize readers with researched-based competencies associated with successful team building. In one study, nearly 100,000 managers representing some of America's leading corporations and government organizations were surveyed in order to identify and validate the abilities, skills, and practices commonly associated with highly effective leaders. These competencies are the "backbone" of this pocket guide.

Reading this book is not a substitute for participation in a formal managerial assessment and improvement program, but familiarity with the competencies presented here will make such program experiences richer. The information on critical managerial competencies and the broader discussion of teams, team building, and teamwork will prepare you to confidently begin the process of building a high-performance team.

Introduction

"Team" is one of countless four-letter words that have been so over-used that their original meaning has been lost. The professional literature and promotional claims of team-building consultants suggest that team building has become an all-purpose, organizational elixir.

Poor productivity? Build a team!

Poor morale? Have a team-building ramble through the woods.

Interpersonal conflict among office staff? Team building will cure it.

Sales sagging? Suspend the sales force from ropes or the face of a rock.

Customer complaints? Try team building to tame tempers.

Why not just deliver a stern lecture on adult behavior and a deep, intramuscular injection of vitamin B-12 to all involved?

Has there ever been more snake oil being sold as a cure-all? There is a legitimate time and place for team building, and there are times when money spent on team building is wasted. In this guide, we will point out those differences and suggest strategies that any manager can use to improve the collective performance of workers and volunteers.

After you read through this book and think about the contents for a couple of days, something important will start to happen: You will feel more empowered to make a positive difference in the lives of many people.

Part One

An Overview of Team-Building Research and Practices

Chapter 1

Pioneers in Team Building

The desired end result of teaching, of training, of behavior modification, and of team building are one and the same: changed behavior.

The goal of each of these activities is to help individuals be more effective in their professional and personal roles, and to better equip them to be contributors at work and in their communities.

In the best of all possible worlds, learning takes, sticks, and endures. People are changed in positive, constructive ways. But too often, what was learned becomes forgotten because *the new behaviors are not reinforced on a consistent basis.* Sooner or later, people will revert to what they've always done because it's comfortable.

It's a waste of money to send people for training unless there is a corporate commitment to reinforce the skills and behaviors learned during the team-building process. Managers should not even consider building teams if they are not willing to commit themselves to following up: to reinforcing, praising, coaching, and insisting that participants in training use and strengthen the new behaviors they have acquired.

This is the dark side of the moon that people in the team-building business don't want to talk about. Far too much team-building training has a half-life of only weeks or months, because managers throw it away. In this chapter, we will look at what we now know about adult learning theory to set the stage for the remainder of the book.

3

Kurt Lewin's Theories

Information about how to increase the effectiveness of people working in groups has been available since 1932, when Kurt Lewin, a German social scientist, accepted a visiting professorship at Stanford. Some of Lewin's original work was on aggression and ways to change behavior so people can live together without force, resistance, and retaliation.[1]

Lewin's research at Stanford, the University of Iowa, and the Massachusetts Institute of Technology became the foundation of a new science that provided conceptual tools to better understand, describe, and *influence* the behavior of people in groups: behavioral science.

One of Kurt Lewin's findings back then, echoed in so much of today's chatter about team building, was that the stronger the "we" feeling in groups, the less aggression there will be. Aggression, he said, is supported by a lot of "I" and "me" feelings that appear to grow out of authoritarian leadership and social structures.

Lewin and his colleagues formed the Research Center for Group Dynamics at MIT. In the beginning, the center's focus was on studying ways to reduce aggression. Over the years, the focus shifted over to studying generic methods for introducing and managing planned change. This greater understanding of group processes became the conceptual foundation of management consulting. In fact, Lewin's findings (mostly unremembered now) form the basis of all successful consulting in the human resource field.

Kurt Lewin is best remembered for his model for *force field analysis*, which holds that the behavior of individuals in groups is maintained by the fields of supporting social force (much like homeostasis in medicine—maintaining a steady

---

state). If behavior is to be changed, Lewin believed, then support for specific behaviors has to be removed or reduced—that is, the "steady state" must be disrupted. As an example, alcoholics are "rewarded" for being drunk in the sense that they get attention from family and friends. When alcoholics want to get sober, they are advised to get a new set of friends. Family members are then taught how to "reward" this new sobriety with their attention and affection.

The concept of a "force field" is perhaps best demonstrated by this experiment: iron filings are sprinkled on a sheet of paper. The paper is lowered over a magnet, and voila! The magnet's field of force is seen in the pattern assumed by the iron filings. Similar patterning has been demonstrated in sociometric research: When skilled observers watch the behavior of people in groups, they can very accurately identify those in the group who are leaders and those in the group who are more isolated (and thus do not have much influence on others).

Lewin came up with a model that is sublime in its simplicity: If you want to change behavior (breaking a smoking habit, for example), then you must modify the individual's field of forces. To support desired change in our smoking example, forces acting on the individual will have to include either strengthening arguments for quitting smoking, or weakening social supports for continuing to smoke. Combining those two tactics creates a persuasive argument for changed behavior (giving up the smoking habit). Graphically, it looks something like this:

FORCES DRIVING CHANGE		FORCES RESISTING CHANGE
Smoking is stupid!	vs.	Smoking makes me feel cool!
Smoking kills!	vs.	I'm going to live forever!
Smoking kills your sex drive!	vs.	I've got plenty to spare!

What does all this have to do with team building? Just about everything. People at work live in a social system full of forces that maintain existing behaviors. Behaviors that don't receive social support and that don't create payoffs for the individual tend to disappear without other causation.

Team building is about changing behaviors to achieve higher levels of productivity or some other behavioral outcome. Remember: Everything we do is behavior, and every choice we make is expressed through behavior.

> Team building is about changing how people think about their work group, its members, the manager, and the company that employs all of them.

The status quo (how things are) is not going to change if the driving forces are not strengthened and the resisting forces are not weakened or devalued. Should a change actually happen and, say, the individual quits smoking, the social-pressure imbalance must be maintained: the driving forces for quitting smoking must be supported and must produce rewards. Otherwise, the original field of forces operating on the individual that prompts him to smoke will regain their strength.

Then the old status quo behavior will return and the individual will smoke.

> Change efforts that fail actually reinforce and strengthen the old behaviors, because the resisting forces have "won."

Lewin must have recognized that it would be difficult for some people to envision how they might be able to maintain social pressure, because he created a second model and made it as elegantly simple as the original, except for the lingo. It looks like this:

Unfreeze → Change → Re-freeze

Operationally, that means destabilizing supports (as in the first model) and moving behavior where you want it to go. Then, once the change has occurred and desired behavior is being observed, you have to "re-freeze" the behavior and the field of forces supporting the change. That re-freezing must be based on forces equal to or greater than those in the original setting in order to lock in the new behavior. And then, following the laws of successful behavior modification, you have to develop a system of periodic but unscheduled rewards to maintain the new behavior.

One of the interesting things about rewards is that they must be immediate and frequent when new behavior is being "set," but they can become more intermittent and unscheduled as behavior continues. Once the desired behavior becomes part of a new pattern of habits, you must continue to reinforce it with "rewards," but it can be done less frequently.

The Beat Goes On

It's obvious that a lot of headwork and homework is required if you are trying to build a sense of teamwork for the future, but this step is usually ignored. People seem to be too busy to plan, to perform according to the plan, and to do the necessary follow up that is required to protect the original investment of time and money in team building or in any other behavior-change effort.

Each successful advertising campaign to launch a new product, each jury-selection process, and each successful attempt to persuade a manager to do something reflects the concepts originally introduced by Kurt Lewin: Someone makes a list of driving forces, forcing people to identify reasons "why we should" and "why we don't want to."

Whether making major sales or defending or promoting a cause, rank-order the items to reflect relative strength in the values held by the people to be convinced; that's where the most compelling arguments need to be crafted. The amount of information developed by a good team that works together can be significant; in fact, the success of the change effort is going to depend on that information.

It takes relatively little time to do a force field analysis, and it produces amazing insights and results. All that is required of you is to think ahead and make data collection and analysis part of your plan.

Kurt Lewin died in 1947, but his work continued when many staff members and the center he established at MIT became part of the University of Michigan's Survey Research Center. The new center was renamed the Institute for Social Research, under the direction of Rensis Likert.

In 1947, the results of one of Likert's research studies were released. There were two central conclusions: One, workers are less-willing to accept pressure and close supervision. Two, supervisors who are employee-centered can get employees to produce more than can supervisors who are job-centered.

By the time Likert published his award-winning work *New Patterns of Leadership* in 1961, he was able to identify 24 characteristics of highly effective work groups. In abbreviated form, here are the characteristics of such groups:

The Characteristics of Highly Effective Work Groups

1. Members are skilled in leadership, as well as in membership roles.

2. Working relationships are relaxed.

3. There is loyalty among members.

4. There is a high degree of confidence and trust.

5. Group values and goals reflect the needs and goals of the group.

6. Individuals are linked through shared values and goals.

7. Individuals adopt the values that are most important to the group.

8. The individuals are highly committed to supporting the group.

9. Respect for individuals is reflected in all problem-solving and decisions.

(Continued)

The Characteristics of Highly Effective Work Groups
(continued)

---

10. The leader models group-building and maintenance behaviors.

11. The group is eager to help individuals achieve maximum potential.

12. Each member is supported in the achievement of personal goals.

13. Expectations are high enough to stretch everyone to excel.

14. Everyone helps and supports one another.

15. Creativity is encouraged and rewarded.

16. All members meet necessary administrative and paperwork requirements.

17. Full and frank communication is the norm.

18. No issue is ignored that is felt to be important by anyone.

19. Feedback on group performance is welcomed by all.

20. Members are encouraged to accept the influence of others.

21. The leader is open to feedback regarding his or her performance.

22. Ideas, attitudes, and goals are not frozen.

23. Members feel confident about making decisions.

24. The leader has been screened carefully (often with peer review).

Truthfully, there's not much to say about effective teams that wasn't said in that 1961 book.[2] What are the fields of force that have kept Lewin's and Lickert's research buried for fifty years? Will they keep you from internalizing and using this information?

Is it possible that two generations of managers have not been able to overcome social pressures restricting performance? Is organizational culture the reason why some managers ignore such down-to-earth information? Is it too abstract? Is it not trusted? Or is it simply that executives and supervisors were and are unwilling to submit to the team-building discipline Likert's findings demand? Perhaps they do not understand the essence of team building because team building has not yet been widely packaged and presented so that real people in real organizations can accept it, adopt it, and implement principles that are universal and proven.

Managerial Competencies

Contemporary researcher Scott Parry took all of Lickert's 24 characteristics and translated them into what he considers major and minor competencies.[3] He validated his conclusions by conducting interviews with thousands of managers. The competencies he identified and "packaged" in his Managerial Assessment of Performance (MAP) include three that are specific to the managerial functions related to building a high-performance team.

The three team-building competencies to master, as identified by Parry, are:

> Appraising People and Performance
> Training, Coaching, and Developing
> Disciplining and Counseling

In the pages that follow, we'll present some insights into organizational and individual issues surrounding teams, teamwork, and team building. As you will see, these three competencies are critical if you want to successfully transform a group into a high-performance team.

Chapter 1 Notes

1. Take some time to review Kurt Lewin's truly seminal work. His concepts are still being examined and developed. Start with his 1997 book, *Resolving Social Conflicts and Field Theory in Social Science* (Washington, D.C.: American Psychological Association).

2. Rensis Lickert's *New Patterns of Management* (New York: McGraw-Hill Book Company) won the Organization Development Council Award for 1961, the McKinsey Foundation Award for 1961-1962, and the James A. Hamilton Hospital Administrators' Award for 1961. Such awards validate the significance of this book and Lickert's work, which was completed nearly 50 years ago. We keep gilding this lily! Truthfully, how much is new since then?

3. Check out Scott B. Parry's 2000 book, *Training for Results: Key Tools and Techniques to Sharpen Trainers' Skills* (Alexandria, Virginia: ASTD Press).

Chapter 2

Understanding Why Workers Do More—and Why They Don't

One of the amazing things we learned from the Civil Rights and Equal Employment Opportunity movements in the United States was that there were people who honestly didn't understand that having a job meant coming to work at 8:00 a.m. five days a week. That kind of time and place discipline was not in their experience: These were adults who had no assigned chores or duties during their developmental years, and no paid work experiences of any kind (other than, for some, farming) that gave meaning to the concept of "going to work." Most of these new employees had only a meager education. Obviously, these individuals needed a lot of extra support and coaching in their first few months of employment if they were to keep their jobs.

There are still people today who finish college without ever having to be responsible for anything more than doing the homework associated with their classes (i.e., no summer jobs, no participation in work-study programs). They arrive at their first job expecting to be treated like the special people their parents have led them to believe they are.

How differently these young people perform from peers who have had many paid and unpaid work experiences throughout their teen and young-adult years. *They* understand what it means to work at a job and be responsible.

Different Strokes for Different Folks

A typical work group will be composed of individuals whose orientation and commitment toward work and the organization lies somewhere along a continuum between two extremes:

Work? Why? ←————————→ I love to work!

Before any kind of team building can begin, managers must level the playing field by creating some common denominator of commitment to and understanding of the tasks, procedures, and processes of the work at hand.

That's not always easy. Gifted lecturer and physician Lee K. Buchanan speaks to managers about the difficulties associated with supervising people. He describes such polar opposites as "San Diego Sammy," who was overindulged by his parents and spent all his free time at the beach with his surfboard; and "New England Nellie," who grew up on a farm in Maine, milking cows and digging potatoes. These two types appear at different ends of the motivational universe. Sammy cannot get enough praise and attention, while all it takes to keep Nellie focused on tasks is just to remember her birthday.[1]

> How do you coach, counsel, train, and discipline people with such a range of orientations toward work? One at a time, and over time.

Tough Love in the Workplace

Being able to train people to be productive workers is the positive side of the coin. On the reverse side are those employees who feel that they have been slighted by their present manager or previous manager, and resent it. Theirs is always a negative voice, quietly undermining any attempts by management to create a positive work environment. And then there are the professional cynics who, with no motivation other than their dark view of life, are given to saying things such as "*That* will never happen!" or "Who does he think he's kidding?" or "Not again! She's handing out the same old stuff!"

Negative energy has a negative impact on work-group morale, impedes team building, and degrades the performance capacity of people who cannot avoid hearing such negative comments. Are these attitude problems? No, they're performance problems: The negative comments and undermining behavior of such people interferes with the performance of others. It's that simple.

Negative people usually perform okay, though probably at the low end of satisfactory. Performance appraisal systems and programs (such as MAP/Excel) can help managers win the contests such employees set up—and this is where a manager's ability to use confrontation pays off. The company has a right to expect people to be good corporate citizens and responsible adults. With a little forethought, the manager can present a negative employee with a clear choice: shape up, or ship out.

High-performance teams require members who are positive, enthusiastic about the work to be done, and supportive of each other. Negative, non-supportive people have to get reoriented— or they have to be replaced.

Process Check: Do you *really* need to build a team?

There are essentially only two kinds of work: routine work, and project work. In most organizations, 80 percent or more of the activities involve routine work—selling things, making things, administering things.

Trying to turn routine, repetitive work into projects causes distortions in the work flow and diminishes the value of project management as an important management tool. It's really just a motivational gimmick, an attempt to get *better, faster, cheaper* performance from people who are smarter than their tasks require them to be. That is, they get bored doing boring work.

There are things managers can do that will relieve the monotony of doing boring work. (Team building is NOT one of them.) Try these things:

- Come into the work area with a cake, shouting "Cake Break!"

- Have brown bag lunches once a month. Invite a senior manager to speak, or show a funny video.

- Remember birthdays or name days, engagements, divorces ("new beginnings" celebrations), and any other reason to take 20 minutes for some fun and fellowship.

- Be honest about the nature of the work, and be creative, upbeat, and real in breaking the monotony.

But if it's your job to supervise people who have to do what is truthfully pretty dumb stuff, don't make it worse by telling them how wonderful it is and trying to pump them up with team-building activities. Please.

By the way, what is the difference between routine work and projects? A project is characterized by five criteria:

1. A project is a unique, one-of-a-kind task.
2. There are specific start and end dates.
3. There are specific technical criteria.
4. There is a budget.
5. There is a client (either internal or external).

The team-building competencies presented in this book are Appraising People and Performance; Training, Coaching, and Developing; and Disciplining and Counseling. They are all needed to enhance performance and appraise it, and to develop individual competencies. What's important is to use these conceptual tools appropriately.

What is routine work? Most administrative and HR tasks that involve the same reports and the same kind of content every week or month are considered routine work. So are most assembly tasks that involve the same work every day, as well as most customer service or patient care work that's based on individual competence and dedication. Your time reading and thinking through the information in this guide will not be wasted, no matter what your role in the organization; it will pay off for you as a manager or a leader.

If you haven't yet considered it and you're in a position to make such a recommendation, think about outsourcing what you think of as "dumb work" to sheltered workshops. It will create exciting projects for handicapped people or people with limited ability who will appreciate the opportunity to do real work and make a few bucks. It will probably reduce your company's costs. In one such experience, a company outsourced a packaging chore to a group of mentally-challenged workers. They were able to complete the task ahead of schedule and on budget—twice. There was no third time, however, because the plant's managers (some of whom had project management training) couldn't manage to get the handicapped workers, the products, and the packaging materials together at the same time.

Consider this insight about your role from a truly unique source: the coffee-roasting manager for the international chain of coffee houses we know as Starbucks:

> Leaders should not think of themselves as simply managers, supervisors, etc., but rather as *team leaders*. Thinking of yourself as a manager or supervisor places you in a position of traditional authority based solely on respect for the position, which places you in a position of power. By understanding the personal work preferences and motivations of your team members, you as an individual, rather than your position, will earn their *real* respect and trust.[2]

Power and the fear it instills in others is the tool of Neanderthal managers. As you begin to consider your role as a team leader, re-think all the stuff you've heard about the privileges of rank and the prerogatives of managers. Those ideas came from the era of authoritarian management, and they don't play too well today.

Maybe you can motivate *your* co-workers into becoming a high-performance team. One of my purposes in writing this book is to assure you that external motivation, for all its purported power, is pretty empty. Motivation has to come from within.

A Motivational Model That Works

The first thing to understand about motivation is the most obvious: You should never try to motivate people who are already doing what you want them to do! You might want to consider giving them incentives to keep doing the right things in the right ways, but you don't need to energize them or push people into action.

> Motivation is always about getting people to do things that they don't want to do. If people like doing something and it makes sense to them, all you need is a little encouragement to keep them at their tasks.

You do not have to motivate children to run in the sun and play football. You do not have to motivate adults in the bars to drink beer and eat chips. You do not have to motivate nuns to pray or teachers to teach or physicians to heal. Maybe there are some new moves in football, some new brands of beer to try, some new litanies to recite, some new protocols/medicines to try, or some new organizational procedures that are worth instituting. You might have to spell out the advantages of doing something differently, but if the changes make sense, people will usually adopt them. Effective sales people already know this.

But suppose the changes do not make sense to the individuals involved? Is it then time for motivation in the form of bribes? Rewards, if they comply? Threats, if they do not? What a waste of money and energy and goodwill!

Getting People to Do What You Want Them to Do

Most managers have to work against the triple constraints of schedule, cost, and quality. There is always the temptation to push workers to meet difficult objectives, but that usually produces anger and resentment. It becomes a self-fulfilling prophecy that actually pushes the workers further away from cooperating and collaborating.

Why get angry? Instead, ask your workers for help.

What follows is a six-step approach to motivation and building cooperative and collaborative relationships with your staff. It will work when everything else fails, but it comes with a price: You will have to approach your workers as peers and colleagues.

A Motivation Model That Works

Step 1: Ask for help! Whether you are reaching out to one person or 10, ask for help. Explain that you have been given a task to accomplish that requires more effort than your own, and tell them that you need their help.

Step 2: Tell them what must be done differently. Any time there is a need to "motivate," you're really trying to get a different outcome (probably using different methods). Workers know this. When you are not honest and up-front in telling them what has to be changed, you feed their mistrust of you and all managers and all organizations. Remember, you are not the first manager to try to outsmart them! The others failed, and so will you unless you change the game and begin by telling the truth.

(Continued)

A Motivation Model That Works (concluded)

Step 3: Tell them why. There is always a reason why something exists or needs to be changed. *We are under pressure to reduce costs* is a good reason for change. *We have been late with this client's deliveries on the past two shipments. If we're late again, we're going to lose the account, and that might put some of your jobs at risk.* That's also a powerful argument.

Step 4: Ask for their input. Many workers say that no manager has ever asked their opinion or asked for their ideas. Others believe that it's a risk even to suggest a different way to do their work. Imagine how surprised your workers will be if you ask them, "What do you think? How can we get this job done a week earlier?" Suppose you collect their ideas and let your workers see that you value their input enough to write their ideas down on an easel without criticizing them. *That* can be a powerful stimulant for extra effort.

Step 5: Develop a plan to get the work done. Using the workers' ideas (and your own), develop an action plan (with their help) and implement it. Of course, if they don't have ideas, you will. But even if your idea is better, remember that you will make more money and progress with your workers by using *their* ideas. This is especially true early on in your effort to develop new ways of working together.

Step 6: Celebrate your successes. When you win your contest against the calendar or the budget, celebrate! Maybe it will be only cake and coffee, but do something to say, *We won!* And while that celebration is in progress, use it as a time to recognize the contributions of individuals, as well as the extra efforts, ideas, and initiatives taken that enabled the team to achieve the results you wanted.

Motivation and What Workers Need

The approach outlined above seems outside orthodox motivational theory, but it is really quite congruent with the approaches of all the "big name" theorists, such as Abraham Maslow. Maslow demonstrated in his "Hierarchy of Needs" that we are not motivated by needs that have already been satisfied, such as job security, but rather by the most immediate need that has not been satisfied.

Frederick Herzberg's "Motivation Hygiene Theory," tested in thousands of real workplaces, proved that managers can get 10 to 15 percent more output from workers just by not making them angry with lies and condescending behavior.

The "master model" is Douglas McGregor's Theory X and Theory Y. [5] Most managers are still in the Theory X camp, believing that workers are a lazy, work-avoiding subclass of people who need to be managed, manipulated, and coerced into producing.

The Theory Y side of the fence: Theory Y managers believe that people can and will solve any problems at work—if they want to. This is where our six-step motivation model fits in.

But what about the workers' position, so often expressed by the statement "Give us more money and we'll do more work"? Workers usually know that you cannot give them more money, but they want you to feel as impotent as they do, so they ask you anyway.

The Truth About Money

Here's the truth about money: Most people in the labor market have a pretty accurate idea how much their skills are worth. Anyone who can make another fifty dollars a day will leave to get the money, and anyone who does not believe he can get a better, more reliable paycheck somewhere else will stay. People at work are very realistic about money. Herzberg discovered this reality 40 years ago through his work in North America, South America, Asia, and Western Europe.

> Money is not the issue in teamwork and team building. Trust and mutual respect are.

There is much in the history of most organizations to cause workers to distrust their managers, and this is often accompanied by mutual disrespect. If your goal is to build more-productive relationships within a team, these two very powerful realities have to be reversed.

The six-step motivation model we introduced in this chapter is a way to get the team-building process started and then to tap into the productive potential residing in the skills and experiences of your workers. The potential is always there. The real question is this: Will managers ask for help?

A Team? Or a High-Performance Team?

How is a *high-performance team* different from any other team? The difference is primarily in the training and skill levels of team members. The combined mastery of tasks permits completion faster than the durations specified by manufacturers or other acknowledged sources of standards. Such advanced performance capabilities produce pride-of-accomplishment among team members that comes from being very good at what they do, and being acknowledged by others as the best in the business.

Successful performance and appreciation for special services builds confidence and—let's admit it—builds the egos of the best performers. Self-perception is very important as an energizer.

In one refinery, a group of specialists spent most of their time sitting around, waiting for the alarm bell. Waiting to repair breakdowns was tough for high-energy guys who really were competent. No wonder their morale was sagging. A slight change in the wording of their mission proved to be the motivational fix. Instead of being there to fix breakdowns, their new charge was to *prevent* breakdowns by using their knowledge of the system and their diagnostic skills to intervene *before* work-stopping breakdowns occurred.

Notice the semantics: Fix breakdowns vs. prevent breakdowns—moving from being reactive to being proactive. The specialists performed many of the same tasks in the preventive-maintenance mode, but they could choose the timing of repairs to minimize impact on workflow and system downtime. Their value to the organization went up dramatically, and so did their morale.

This particular team's performance validates the widespread belief that *training, coaching, and delegating* are competencies of high-performance managers. Their manager knew there was something going on within the team, but neither he nor the team members could figure out what was pulling down their morale. However, this manager had the courage to ask for help from an outsider who could see through the macho culture and "tradition" to diagnose the source of the team's discontent.

High-performance teams develop the ability to respond quickly to requests for support, and perform well against tight deadlines. They set standards for themselves and take pride in trying to meet or exceed their own standards.

> Being a member of a high-performance team means being able to perform at levels that are a lot more than okay.

Is high-performance teamwork possible in a 9-to-5 office, with its repetitive routines driven by legal procedures and forms? Of course. The driving force is not team-building, however, but normal conventions of courtesy and common sense: People who understand their roles, their tasks, and the requirements to work together in specified ways will perform, unprompted and without pressure, because it makes sense. When what makes sense *isn't* happening, look for the reasons: Nine times out of ten, you will find the cause of breakdowns to be interpersonal stuff—rudeness or other behavior that causes bad feelings. Those things can and should be addressed, but never use team building to do it.

Conceptual tools are no different from carpenters' tools; use them correctly, and only for their intended purposes.

Chapter 2 Notes

1. Lee K. Buchanan was medical director at the U. S. Department of Agriculture and a frequent lecturer at seminars organized by the author. His thesis was about the enormous pressure often imposed on managers by their employers to make decisions contrary to their values; the physical and psychological stresses that resulted; and coping strategies.

2. Don Clark, a training specialist while in the U.S. Army, created *Big Dog's Leadership Page* in 1997, and continues to make available an extensive and readable presentation about organization, management, and leadership principles. Check it out at http://www.nwlink. com /~donclark/index.html. As you will see, *Big Dog* knows his stuff.

3. Abraham Maslow was a charismatic figure in the field who had a large following of clinicians and managers. His 1965 book, *Eupsychian Management: A Journal* (Irwin-Dorsey) was based on his summer as a researcher-in-residence at Non-Linear Systems, a San Diego high-tech manufacturing firm. It was Maslow's first experience in an industrial setting, and the notes from his journal are the basis for the book. More great insights from the past.

4. Frederick Herzberg was the author of *The Managerial Choice: To Be Efficient and to Be Human* (New York: Dow Jones-Irwin, 1976). Herzberg believed that we are driven by two factors: the need to avoid pain, and the need to grow psychologically. These factors do not represent conflicting values, so it is possible to be effective without creating pain for others. His findings have been replicated in a wide variety of cultural and organizational settings. Read about him to get a deeper understanding of how relevant his research is today. Another blast from the past.

5. Douglas McGregor is the author of the seminal book *The Human Side of Enterprise* (New York: McGraw Hill Book Company, 1960). This is *the* source of all contemporary management theory! McGregor's work was derided by some as too philosophical and soft-headed, but the technological advances he anticipated, along with the need for corporate management to make major shifts in treatment of human resources, make this book an invaluable text. Get to know this author and his work.

Chapter 3

Performance Improvement As a Political Process

The laws of life operate in the workplace, just like every-where else. You really do catch more flies with honey and than with vinegar, and it really is easier to do something special for someone you like than for someone you don't care about.

Managers who are popular with workers tend to be more effective and productive than their counterparts. They are also given more special assignments and invitations to attend meetings with executive-level people than other managers.

When you look closely at any manager's success, how-ever, you notice that a big part of it comes about because the workers want their boss to succeed. Workers "vote." When it's quitting time and a task is nearly finished, people who work for a manager they respect and trust are much more likely to say, "What the hell. Let's finish this tonight instead of letting if drift over until tomorrow." That's a "yes" vote for the manager. On the other hand, workers who don't like their manager are likely to say something like, "Screw it. If he wants it finished tonight, let him do it himself!"

Voting Is Never Secret for Long

Over time, those "yes" and "no" votes matter. In fact, manag-ers who don't get much from their people because they aren't liked and respected will be noticed in short time by *their* managers.

That's the difference between groups of isolated workers and a bona fide team: With a team, there's so much positive energy that a kind of synergy is created. When you put out positive energy, you also pull in positive energy that is put out from others, and it will be invested in completing tasks on time or ahead of schedule. In extremely effective teams, an energy-multiplier effect takes place. Consider the impact of that kind of synergy on a team's productivity!

> If you put out positive energy you will pull in positive energy from others.

The "secret," if there is one, is in the positive worker-manager dynamic, which develops when the team leader models the behavior and the kinds of verbal responses that will permit the team's synergy to form.

Positive Feelings, Positive Energy, Positive Results

There's a lot of psychobabble associated with team building, so let's be clear about what it's not supposed to do: The purpose is *not* to make people feel better about themselves, but rather to enable them to perform assigned tasks better, faster, and cheaper so that the employing organization can meet its goals.

If your goal is for people to feel good about themselves, set them up to perform a task that is challenging but do-able, and encourage them in the process of doing their work. When they succeed (which they will), celebrate. Make them feel like local heroes. Then roll off that success with another challenge, and then another. Always end with celebrations, and the positive energy you want to see will be there. There's no substitute for success as a basis for enhanced self-esteem. When groups of people are feeling good about themselves, positive energy will surround them. Just remember one thing: Any group of workers can be made more effective if you use the energy-building techniques mentioned above, but an energized work group is not a team. It can quickly lose its energy, and this is when people will revert to their old ways of being with and relating to each other and to their assigned tasks. It's the team leader's responsibility to keep this energy-field going.

The Critical Element in Team Formation

The one element that is absolutely essential when you are trying to develop a productive work team is commitment: Commitment to the team's successful performance of assigned tasks. Commitment to the success of the team and its members. Commitment to the employing organization.

When we feel important and believe that our work is necessary to the group, we commit to it. We need and want to work with the rest of our team members, and we feel good when something good happens to them. But sometimes there are limits. Consider this result of a team-building process that was conducted with the staff of a major zoological park.

By any standard, this particular zoological park was and is an interesting and beautiful place to work. There was a time in recent years when the zoo director was concerned that while things were okay with the staff, people had never really come together as the kind of team he wanted.

He brought in a consultant who paid a visit to each member of the professional staff in their work places. He used the same interview protocol with each of them, and soon, the "problem" became obvious. The consultant was not sure it could be solved, however (at least in terms of getting the "team feeling" the director wanted).

A Saturday retreat was scheduled so the consultant could present his interview findings. The group arrived at the meeting room and saw this on a flipchart:

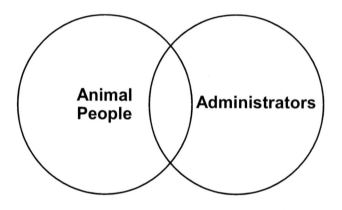

Two overlapping circles of about equal size were drawn on the chart, one labeled "Animal People" designating the veterinarians and their assistants and the animal behavior specialists. The other circle, "Administrators," designated the HR manager, purchasing manager, and other administrators. The overlapping area represented only two people who fit into both circles: the director, and the manager of maintenance (a retired soldier who said, "This is the best job in town for me.").

Everyone knew that the animal people were committed to the animals. Sitting up late into the night with a birthing gnu was not unusual. Where else could they work, except in another zoo?

The administrators, on the other hand, possessed transferable skills, so they could move to another agency without any retraining. The people in this group were always willing to consider a better job offer.

To the outsider, the two-orbit organization made perfect sense. Happily, the participants were able to see the logic, once they got past the feeling that they were being labeled or blamed or demeaned by being bunched together as though they were in separate organizations (which, in fact, they had become).

In the several hours of conversation that followed, the group was able to identify ways to work together more effectively and to communicate more sensitively with people whose heads were really in a different place. The outcome of the retreat was a better understanding of the motives and passions of the animal people by the administrators, and a reciprocal appreciation of the support provided to the park and its mission by the administrators. The two groups had never really talked before!

When they confronted this two-circle reality and all the defensiveness was drained away, there was a sense of relief around the room. One of the vets said, "I knew there was something that didn't fit about how we worked together, and it bothered me. Sometimes I even thought it was personal. Now that I see what it is—we really are in different orbits. And that's okay!"

There was a similar sense of relief among the administrators, because they realized why they had felt excluded by the animal people. It turned out that it wasn't so much that they had been excluded as that they never bothered to be part of the midnight vigils or other animal-focused episodes. The two groups would never become a tight team in the usual sense: a group of people united by similar skills and interests. However, after the retreat, they became a better working group— they were more respectful of each other as professionals, but with very different orientations. By all accounts, the retreat was a success.

Sometimes managers and teams have to make interesting and intelligent compromises. Not every group can become a team; in such situations it would not be constructive to create pressures for conformity. When there is a frenzy in an organization for team building, it's often a response to a fad ("Everyone is wearing black this winter"). The evolution of American management has been described by some as a kind of hopscotch, with theoretical fads of the month becoming the stepping stones leading away from the simple and workable constructs provided by Kurt Lewin and Rensis Likert.

Tom Peters sparked one of the neatest business fads: Management by walking around. Peters is one of the greatest innovators in the field of management, and he believed that managers should get out on the plant floor to chat with workers and get feedback from the bottom up. Before long, managers in every industry were taking time each day to see for themselves how things were going.

One manager and his consultant were talking about ways to overcome the ineptitude of the organization's politically appointed director. The consultant wondered aloud, "What about MBWA for him?" "A waste of time," said the manager. "He wouldn't know what he was looking at!"

There are two morals to this story: The first is that no fad or approach works for everyone. The second is that it's difficult to be an effective team leader unless you know quite a lot about your team and the technologies they use (your other competencies notwithstanding).

Assessment programs that use research-based managerial competencies (such as MAP) are not fads; they will be helping people become more skilled and proficient for decades to come.

Chapter 3 Note

1. Thomas J. Peters and Robert H. Waterman's *In Search of Excellence: Lessons from America's Best-Run Companies* (Harper/Collins, 1982) was rated as "the best business book of all time" in a poll taken by Britain's Bloomsbury Publishing in 2002. Pick up a used copy. Great reading, and the launching pad for a number of other books by Peters and his far-reaching consultancy.

Chapter 4

Developing Leaders in Your Teams

Research into group effectiveness tells us that every successful group needs people who call the plays and people who can keep the energy flowing. A leader of an effective group is an individual who performs a number of necessary roles to keep the group moving effectively toward outcomes and decisions.

These roles have historically been described as *task functions* and *maintenance functions,*[1] but some researchers have added *hindering functions.*[2] Since the original list contains only constructive roles, why not identify the destructive behaviors as well? Here is an abbreviated list of the roles and behaviors we often see in groups:

Task Functions

- *Initiating:* Proposing ideas that launch or maintain discussion.
- *Information- or opinion-seeking:* Asking for supporting information.
- *Information- or opinion-giving:* Providing input.
- *Clarifying or elaborating:* Interpreting ideas, giving examples.
- *Summarizing:* Pulling comments together, offering a conclusion.
- *Consensus testing:* Checking for agreement.

Maintenance Functions

- *Encouraging:* Being complimentary, giving recognition to others.
- *Expressing group feelings:* Sensing and expressing the mood of the group.
- *Harmonizing:* Smoothing-over, reconciling disagreements.
- *Compromising:* Looking for a middle ground to resolve conflict.
- *Gate-keeping:* Bringing silent members into the discussion.
- *Setting standards:* Asking "Is this the best we can do?"

Hindering Functions

- *Dominating:* Appearing authoritative, over-communicating.
- *Withdrawing:* Becoming non-participative.
- *Degrading:* Making disrespectful or discouraging comments.
- *Uncooperative:* Blocking, using hidden agendas to frustrate progress.
- *Side conversations:* Private chatter, giggling, showing attention.

Real Issues and Real Behaviors
That Impact Performance

All of the behaviors in the list, including the hindering ones, usually emerge in a group meeting lasting 30 minutes or more. Some people perform two or more task or maintenance functions, usually contributing to the group's movement toward a successful completion of the meeting. *The exception is in authoritarian settings where no one speaks except the designated manager.*

Early researchers sought to identify group behaviors to demonstrate what people do when they are committed to the team and the work it's doing. Some of these behaviors are spontaneous, but most are more likely to appear when everyone understands what the roles are and how necessary they are to keep the team moving toward success. They tend to be most frequent when members are so involved in the team's process that they lose their self-consciousness about participating and speak up about what they feel or see.

How do you create that understanding of task and maintenance functions? One way is to have a discussion, with everyone reading from the same handouts. But more learning will take place when there is an observer who periodically points out specific behaviors as they are happening. The observer might say something like:

> Let me interrupt. Did you notice what Dick did just a moment ago? He asked Sally a direct question that she had to answer. That got her back into the discussion, because she hasn't said anything for 20 minutes. That's a perfect example of gate-keeping.

When group/team members participate in this kind of live tutorial and see the behaviors identified in the context of a real meeting, the 12 positive actions cease to be academic distinctions, and make more sense, as will the five hindering behaviors.

The manager/team leader can use the last few minutes of the meeting to summarize the content of the meeting and note how well people interacted during the meeting. That way, they reinforce the importance of the helping roles and encourage people to use them.

As a further step, the manager/team leader should speak privately after the meeting with one or several people whose contributions were significant in helping to "set" the behavior so there will be more of it. Committed team builders must consistently reinforce the behavior they want.

Why is this important? Because many managers prefer an authoritarian-type, talk-down-to meeting (and this is what employees are used to). After all, telling people what to do takes less time than participating, at least initially. Managers also tend to fear losing control of a meeting. *(What if everyone talks at once? What if no one listens? What if there are arguments and disagreements? Suppose there is angry conflict?)*

Members of a disciplined team take care of those issues themselves, using the task and maintenance functions to support the group's process. This will eventually become natural for them because it is their team, their task, their time, and their eagerness to succeed.

If any of the hindering behaviors are displayed, team members will prove quite capable of dealing with them quickly, if not always kindly. ("Joe, shut up! You're over-communicating again!")

Group members are peers, so there aren't usually any authority issues. They can be painfully direct with one another. Obstructive individuals will often change their behavior more quickly when they get straight feedback from a peer than when they are critiqued politely by the manager.

By relinquishing the authoritarian role, managers and team leaders invite and make room for constructive, supportive participation from team members, but they won't relinquish the traditional authoritarian role unless and until they trust team members to be responsible adults.

Training, Coaching, and *Delegating* are important competencies possessed by all effective managers. They are proactive competencies in the sense that groups cannot become teams unless someone provides the training, does the quiet coaching, and trusts people enough to delegate and invite their participation.

A Simple Training Model

San Francisco coffee merchant Luciano Repetto has developed and maintained a really competent customer-service staff. After many visits over the years to Graffeo's Coffee Roasting Company I finally asked Luciano how he does it—how he gets such a high level of performance out of people. He described his personal training program:

- First, you **tell** people what you want them to do.

- Second, you **show** them how to do it.

- Third, you **test** them to make sure that they know what to do and how to do it.

- Fourth, you **check** their performance—frequently at first, to be sure the work is being done properly and to make corrections. Then, periodically, forever!

The world's simplest training model:

Tell! Show! Test! Check!

What could be simpler? But do notice the last word in that training model: Forever. If there's no "Follow up forever" in your training plan, pretty soon performance will slip to the point where someone says, "You'd better get these people back into training." Several pages back, I talked about managers who "throw away" training. Forgetting the *forever* is the way it happens.

No matter how elite the team is, you have to supervise it, assess results, coach, and fine-tune the team's performance through short-term targets for improvement. This must be ongoing and done with seriousness and consequences. Otherwise....

"Disciplining" is knowing how to discipline people to get their performance back within standards. It is widely considered to be a managerial competence, but there is no standard of "discipline" for managers—that is, for follow-up and follow-through, and for doing the dogged work of maintaining worker performance. Sadly, a lot of managers seem not to have the stomach or the attention span for that part of the job. I hope you will.

Chapter 4 Note

1. Descriptions of task and maintenance functions have not changed much over the years. These have been taken from a 1965 compilation of booklets titled *"The Looking into Leadership Executive Library,"* published by the consulting firm Leadership Resources, Inc. of Washington, D.C. One of the first behaviorally-oriented consulting firms in the country, its founders included such training luminaries as Gordon Lippitt and Leonard Nadler.

Chapter 5

Using Subject-Matter Experts to Make Participative Management Work

An authoritarian manager believes that he or she is supposed to know how to do everything better than the employees. In an era of simple technologies, that was probably possible, but nowadays, it's the lucky manager who is even conversant with all the technologies employed by workers in the organization.

Enter the subject-matter expert. He or she won't necessarily be a manager; in fact, the SME might be a recent university graduate with little organizational work experience. But when there is a discussion about the subject-matter expert's area of expertise, doesn't it make sense to have the person with the most recent and the most relevant experience lead the discussion?

Here's an example of what I mean: Suppose you have an appendicitis attack. The surgery is not something that requires a world-class surgeon, but who would you prefer to have operating on you? A physician who performs 10 or 15 appendectomies a month, or one who says, "I haven't seen an appendix in five years." Most of us would go for the doc with the recent and relevant experience.

Some managers cannot bear to transfer power or leadership even temporarily, to someone with the most recent and relevant experience. They don't want to be upstaged or send the wrong signal to others (who might also try to take the lead). However, such insecurity is becoming rarer as the managerial dinosaurs retire. But do watch the behavior of some of the new, young managers: Many get seduced into becoming an "authority" and an authoritarian manager. For people who know the work they have been doing for years, there are few things more disagreeable than having some brash kid behaving like a tyrannical order-giver.

Using Your Subject-Matter Experts

How can subject-matter experts help the organization? Consider this scenario:

A committee has been organized to plan a "friends and family" picnic for the entire department. The committee chair clipped a list of activity ideas from a magazine article. "Has anyone ever been on a scavenger hunt?" she asks.

A colleague who has participated in scavenger hunts speaks up and describes how to organize and execute the scavenger hunt. He or she will probably be assigned responsibility for putting the hunt together for the entertainment of the 40 children expected to be at the picnic.

Makes a lot of sense, doesn't it? The manager is ultimately responsible, but can assign authority for certain actions to others. Why should he or she try to hold on to a task that someone else can probably do better, faster, cheaper? And why should a manager miss the opportunity to give an employee a little independent responsibility and a chance to show what he/she can do?

When you have an effective team, staff meetings will be run a little differently. Outsiders might be confused about the identity of the designated leader, because that role will change as the subject changes: Each person on the team is considered to be a subject-matter expert and is designated as the lead person on some project or assignment. Everyone is producing and reporting; no one is taking a free ride!

This brings us to another team-building competency: *Delegating.* How else will you ever know if others are competent, unless you give them tasks to perform or sub-groups to lead? Unless you describe what you want (and by when) and which resources are available *and* turn people loose to get assigned tasks done, you'll never know for sure.

Ensuring Success

Delegating isn't about throwing people into deep water to see if they will swim or drown. There is an important developmental point to remember: *Set people up to succeed!*

> People don't learn the most from mistakes. To the contrary: People learn best and fastest from a series of successes.

Here's another part of coffee-roaster Repetto's team-building advice: "Never tolerate a mistake. If you tolerate a mistake, you tell people that making mistakes is okay. It isn't! If you tolerate one mistake, why not two or three or more? Then all of a sudden, you don't have standards anymore."

Standards are absolutely necessary for effective teams and effective workplaces. Standards are a prerequisite for delegation.

Is there a secret to delegation? If there is, it probably would read like this:

Part 1: Start people off with small, clear tasks at which they cannot possibly fail. Reward successful completion. Subsequent tasks will be more complex, but every success will be rewarded. That's how you build confidence in people to do things on their own, to be effective, and to become significant contributors to the team's success.

Part 2: Always provide oversight while delegated work is in progress. Touch base with people. Ask, "How's it going? Are you going to be ready to present your report on Friday?"

This is *not* about control. Instead, it's about being able to find out early on whether or not there are problems so you can prevent failure. What do people learn from failure? What they forgot or never learned before they learned that they were not prepared to succeed. Back to Repetto's point: If you allow people to fail, you have lost twice: First, the work has to be redone. Second, the individual's self-confidence sags and he or she becomes less reliable.

Chapter 6

Success Begets Success

Self-confidence that is validated is a springboard for more productivity, for larger areas of independent action, and for learning how to coach and develop others. When people fail, they look bad in front of their co-workers and become ashamed or embarrassed. If employees feel sand-bagged by assignments and believe that they would never have succeeded anyway, they'll surely feel resentful, releasing dark energies into the group. Then everyone loses. That's why it is so important that a group succeed at what it takes on. This might be the manager's most challenging role: to ensure success.

Developing People Is a Process

Wouldn't it be great if every member of the team were a subject-matter expert? Wouldn't it be fun to work with a really skilled, knowledgeable, competent group of individuals?

Maybe you already do. Chances are good that each of your co-workers has a unique set of skills and abilities that can be called into play to support the team—nascent abilities and things they like to do but don't yet do well. If those latent talents can be brought to the surface and developed, then everyone would have at least two areas of competence. This might also create an opportunity for you to cross-train members of the team so they can act as back-ups for one another. In the process of learning to work together more effectively, they might come to appreciate each other more, thus strengthening the interpersonal "glue" that bonds team members.

Realistically, most organizations are not preoccupied with training, and it is not the central preoccupation of managers. But none of the positive organizational accomplishments we've been talking about can be achieved without some training, and that's why *training* is a managerial competency.

> Employees have to take an active role in their own training and development. It is not something to be done "to" them; they have to want to acquire new skills, abilities, and competencies.

The manager's first training goal should be to start paying attention to people: to listen to and watch them to get an idea of who they are, what they want to learn or improve, and where they want to go in the organization. Then, when it's time to sit down and talk about individual development, the manager can offer comments such as "I've noticed that you often…. Is that something you'd like to do more of?"

With that kind of opening, the individual will find it easier to discuss his or her interests and aspirations. If the individual and the manager can identify ways to use those interests to be more productive at work, you have the beginnings of a plan.

Surprisingly, even very competent people don't always know what they want for themselves, short- or long-term. Here's a way to check that out: The next time you hold a staff meeting, say this:

"I want each of you to get out a sheet of paper. On it, I want you to write down 25 things you want to do in the next 6 months, on the job or on your own time. You don't have to show the list to anyone, not even me. I will give you 15 minutes to complete the assignment. Please let me know when you are finished."

Try this yourself before you continue with the chapter. Give yourself no more than 15 minutes.

25 Personal Goals for the Next Six Months

1. _____
2. _____
3. _____
4. _____
5. _____
6. _____
7. _____
8. _____
9. _____
10. _____
11. _____
12. _____
13. _____
14. _____
15. _____
16. _____

(Continued)

25 Personal Goals for the Next Six Months (concluded)

17. _____
18. _____
19. _____
20. _____
21. _____
22. _____
23. _____
24. _____
25. _____

Some people will complete the assignment in four or five minutes, while others will complete it in 10 or 15 minutes. Some people won't finish, explaining that their goals are very complex. Nevertheless, I have found this to be a useful loosening-up exercise that can also be used to work with a team on personal development. You might notice that a few people you thought were the best and brightest are brain-locked, and others you weren't too sure about have a good idea about what they want to do.

People develop powerful insights as they work through this simple exercise (i.e., *"That's what my wife's been trying to tell me,"* or *"I think I'm in the wrong business"*).

A variant of the exercise is to get the team to develop a list of 25 things members can do to make their work and workplace more pleasant. Or something like that. It's a non-threatening, non-invasive way to find out what people see and think, and it's a good way to initiate constructive action.

Think about what's on your own list. If most of the things you list are about work or family or duties and obligations, that's useful information. And if you have difficulty thinking of 25 things you want to do in the next 26 weekends and you didn't list anything to do with having fun, you might be stuck.

> It's hard to plan itineraries for people who don't know where they want to go. Managers can help an individual create a development plan, but the individual must lead the effort and feel a sense of ownership.

Continuing Development

Life is a process. So is maturing, and so is learning. Maybe an ideal state of being is to stay in the process *of becoming*—becoming more knowledgeable, becoming more skilled, becoming more articulate, becoming more sensitive, becoming more experienced. Isn't that what development is all about—becoming *more* and *better*? It doesn't matter what part of our life we improve, as long as a process of improvement is underway. Becoming better at something in any of life's arenas has carry-over benefits in other areas of our lives, including work.

We should all have a development plan and a partner—someone who will keep us honest by checking to see that all the things we proposed to do actually happen, and that hoped-for learnings actually result.

And now about the plan itself: Too often, development plans are like New Year's resolutions—made with great resolve, but soon forgotten. How many people actually write their resolutions down and post them where they can be seen frequently, if not daily?

Whether it's a list of work skills to acquire or a list of family resolutions, it should be posted where it can be seen easily so people can check off the items as they are accomplished. This creates a sense of momentum; people who have felt "dead in the water" will soon feel rejuvenated and in control of their lives again when they see that they are accomplishing things.

So, when team building is what you want to do, get everyone into the process of learning how to do something better. Hold brown-bag luncheon meetings once a week to discuss books or articles relevant to your business. Get someone to meet with your team to talk about corporate goals, successes, technical breakthroughs, and the impact on employees. Almost any subject will do to get people engaged in something other than last night's TV shows or the next football game. But be realistic: Not every group is going to be transformed into a learning community, but you can do many things as a manager that lead to constructive actions that strengthen the team. Consider this simple real-life example:

> A group of employees started talking about how nice it would be to have an outdoor lunch and break room. Many of them were amateur carpenters, so they began planning a do-it-themselves project. The HR manager contributed a picnic table and benches, their own manager contributed five gallons of paint, and someone else contributed wooden fencing. The group of employees came in on a weekend and managed to convert an unused space in the loading area into the outdoor area they wanted.

They expressed a need and were given the materials, and the result of their planning and volunteer labor was something that exceeded everyone's expectations—including their own. They took the initiative and found themselves empowered—an unexpected yet positive outcome.

It was the beginning of a real transformational experience: This somewhat disgruntled group of employees eventually grew into a high-performance team because of the sense of cohesiveness they developed simply by planning and executing their own project.

Transformational experiences present themselves in a variety of forms. Most often they are personal, often triggered in unexpected ways. Consider this next true story about a project-management seminar in San Francisco:

A presenter was talking about the project manager's duty to create and maintain positive expectations, a source of success-producing energy, when a participant stood up to speak. He held up the aluminum cane with the wrist braces that he used to get around. Here is what he said:

All my life, I've been a cripple. There were so many things I couldn't do that I quit trying. Then someone said, Why don't you go jump out of an airplane? I thought it was another put-down. Still, I thought about it and decided I would do it. I felt so defeated by life that I felt I had nothing to lose by taking such a risk.

I can tell you, I was scared! Up to that point, I had never done anything physically challenging. But I did it! When I felt that parachute snap open and knew I was going to live, my life was changed. That part of me that was a cripple is now gone. I work out with weights, I've learned to ski. I've even tried rock climbing. There's nothing I can't do!

There were nearly 100 people in that room, and they all stood and applauded. Such dramatic moments don't come along every day, but when people get into the process of becoming something more than they are, anything can happen.

Releasing Human Potential for Profit

When a manager wants a participative group of peers instead of passive subordinates, he or she will have to get people to buy into it. They are more likely to do this if their expertise has been recognized and they have been identified as "subject-matter experts." Then they will know that they have a right to speak, and that when they do, others will listen. They will also feel confident that what they say will be received positively because others consider them to possess expertise in a specific area. There is, in fact, a kind of peerage around the conference table when everyone is a subject-matter expert.

Building a team benefits everyone, personally and professionally, but expect there to be obstacles. Too often, managers fail to see the full potential of groups of employees. Tradition and precedent blinds them from seeing the possibilities. Managers from the old Theory X school create a negative self-fulfilling prophecy that says, *"These people cannot and will not do more than they have done in the past."* Sure enough, those employees will do exactly what their managers expect!

This kind of thinking costs employers billions of dollars in potential revenue every year. Practical experience tells us time and time again that when managers ask employees for help in solving problems, problems get solved, productivity goes up, and costs go down. When managers *reward* employees for cost-saving or productivity-improving ideas, they get a steady stream of labor-saving, profit-making suggestions in return. Their employees can then become the company's secret weapon in the price/quality war with competitors.

Let's admit one thing: It's not easy to convince managers that those who do the work always know better, faster, and cheaper ways to do it. It's just as hard to get employees to volunteer ideas and suggestions; they assume that their managers don't want to know or that there will be a backlash of some kind for speaking out.

Managers and employees are vulnerable to self-defeating attitudes. Unprofitable companies disappear every day, as do the jobs. Everyone loses when human potential is ignored in favor of short-term profits, prejudice, old ideas about manager/worker relationships, managers' fears about asking for help, and employees' fears about being punished for thinking.

> Team building is an accelerated approach to releasing human potential.

Releasing human potential is a major responsibility of HR professionals: They need to recognize an individual's potential for contribution and then explain it to managers. Managers should, in turn, ask for and reward participative problem solving. Try it. It's profitable.

Managers: Take a trust walk with your people.

Team builders can use any number of not-so-subtle and more-authoritarian concepts, alongside those we've just described, to get people in gear and going. Here are five of them:

1. *Take charge.* Don't be embarrassed to be the boss. Tell people your understanding of the group's role and purpose, what your expectations are, what your experience is, where you have worked (if you are new to them), and what kinds of results you want and when.

2. *Ask for participation—and mean it.* The people sitting around the table represent an enormous pool of knowledge, talent, experience, street smarts, and energy. They can support you and contribute to your success, or they can do exactly what you tell them and nothing more. A stark contrast, but workers make those decisions the first time they meet a new manager. The test for them is in how the manager treats them. No employee wants to be treated as a subordinate or someone who is less than who they truly are.

   Most people want to be peers and colleagues. Rank and hierarchy exist, but managers who trade on them usually alienate employees at all levels. If you want access to what team members know and you want their support and the results they can deliver, allow them to become colleagues, and involve them in the technical and administrative decisions that affect how they do the team's work.

3. *Establish standards.* A starting point for participation is to establish standards about how you will work together. Tell people what you expect. Ask them what they expect from you. Develop a *reasonable* set of standards for punctuality and workplace discipline, for communicating and conducting themselves at meetings, and for raising and resolving issues.

Here's a simple scheme that will give team members autonomy over their work. Tell them you are breaking reportable information into these three groups:

- *Group A:* Do these things, and let me know what you did. (Probably 80 percent of actions fall into this category.)

- *Group B:* Let me know immediately when you take these kinds of (specified) actions. (About 15 percent of actions will be in this group.)

- *Group C:* Do not do these (specified) things without prior permission. (About 5 percent of potential actions fall into this category.)

This method cannot be used until the manager and all team members understand *at a high level of detail* the nature of the work being done and the organizational context in which they are working. Once everyone understands these things and signs on to this reporting agreement, they can operate with a great deal of autonomy and effectiveness.

4. *Tell the truth.* Managers rarely get away with misleading employees, because too many people have too much information. Perhaps the most frequent test of truth-telling comes when senior management orders something to be done that everyone thinks is stupid. How should the manager respond?

   It's not a good idea for a manager to criticize senior managers. In fact, it can be career death to be quoted as having said things that sound insubordinate. (And such comments usually make their way up the ladder.) Instead, you can say, "This is what I have been told to accomplish, and this is what we will do. With your help, perhaps we can make a better outcome than we expect."

   Likewise, be honest with individuals about their performance, about your expectations, about their need to improve, and about the limits of your ability to support them.

5. *Reward your people and be their advocate.* Unfortunately, many managers do not take care of their people. What a mistake! Workers have the power to make the manager successful. It is an abuse of the company's resources not to take care of the employees—just as bad as standing in the street tearing up $100 bills, or leaving expensive tools or equipment out in the rain to rust. When people know their efforts are not appreciated, they reduce their output to the allowable minimum. That creates a morale problem for formerly conscientious employees, and keeps the organization from using the full range of their abilities and talents. Employees know which managers represent them and their interests, and which ones don't.

Chapter 6 Note

1. The *Managing to Excel* workbooks that are part of the *Management Assessment of Proficiency* (MAP) program contain forms for development planning and other competence-building activities. For more information, contact www.traininghouse.com.

Summing Up Part One

Employees whose managers don't appreciate their contributions, don't reward them, and don't become their advocate for raises or other benefits feel a little differently about going to work than the rest of us: it is just a painful necessity.

You cannot build high-performance teams without first opening up communication channels and creating operating structures that fit the team, its mission, and the organizational setting. Team building is neither easy nor quick. It's never a one-time effort, either. It has to be self-sustaining, because when the consultants leave, it's the manager who must take up the dance. The manager—essentially the team leader—is the one who winds the team-building clock and creates the conditions that make it possible to deliver on-time, on-budget results, predictably and reliably.

Part Two will look more closely at the team leader's role.

Part Two
The Team Leader's Role

Chapter 7
Personal Learning

Building a high-performance team is possible if the leader possesses the right mix of competency and ability, as well as patience, energy, and discipline. The last three criteria are not really teachable per se, but an individual who wants to acquire these traits badly enough can become more patient, more energetic at work, and more disciplined through their own program of personal improvement.

There are other factors associated with individual achievement, such as a person's priorities and degree of commitment, drive, and passion. These variables will not be dealt with here. Instead, we'll focus on competency development. There are at least three stages of personal competency:

1. Familiarity with ("I have heard of them and know they exist.")

2. Knowledge about ("I understand what they mean and can discuss them intelligently.")

3. Ability to perform ("I can do these things against standards, and teach others to do them as well.")

We use the term *competence* to refer to the ability to perform against standards, subject to personal variables. Reading this book can provide familiarity with and knowledge about the competencies to be discussed. The information can help you if you want to work at becoming a team builder and make a difference in the lives of many people, or simply be able to discuss the process articulately.

If you want to become a team builder, the information on the pages that follow will point the way. You can do it if you have the will to do so.

To make the transition from manager to team leader, you must have a "go do it" attitude, a good understanding of people at work, and familiarity with research on the positive economic consequences of participative management.

The goal of the organization is about generating more-profitable performance, and this must also be the team's ultimate goal.

Self-Selected Improvement Tasks

We have a half-century of evidence from actual workplaces that participative management pays off, but there is still some resistance to the idea. Let's try to clear up some of these commonly-held misperceptions about participative management.

Misperception #1: Participative management weakens the manager's role and reduces output.

This is totally wrong. Participative management allows managers to be more effective, produce more output, and contribute to putting more profit on the company's bottom line.

Misperception #2: Participative management is the same as "democratic" management, which means that workers can tell managers what to do.

Workplace "democracy" is not the issue. *Participation* is the issue—getting your employees to work with their managers and with each other more effectively, using their experience to find better, faster, cheaper ways to get work out the door, and bringing job-protecting profit into the company.

Misperception #3: Our workers are used to strict management, and they will do as little as they can unless authoritarian managers are there to push them.

That kind of authority has not produced results in the past; why do you think more of the same will work now? The fact is that in most instances, it is the managers who maintain the distance between themselves and their workers. It is natural for workers to want to contribute by working with their managers to achieve worthwhile goals when managers allow them to participate. Knowing about participation gives managers this production-improving information so they can choose to become more effective instead of more authoritarian (and ineffectual).

Misperception #4: It takes authority to make people work and to get work out the door. Weak managers cannot survive here.

There is always some degree of authority in a supervisory or managerial role. Strength comes from intelligent use of resources; so make it easy for people to do what you want them to do. Otherwise, workers will figure out the least amount of work they have to do, and despite your authority, you will only get that much output. The participative approach has been used in some of America's most challenging workplaces, and it will work in your company, too.

Misperception #5: Participation means a lot of time-wasting conversations about how work should be done, with the dumbest employees talking the most and the smart ones keeping their mouths shut.

Involving workers in making decisions about the work they do might take a little longer initially, but over time it will prove to be a productive use of your time.

There are many other reasons why leaders are reluctant to adopt participative management, but these are some of the more commonly cited. Once you understand what it is, how to implement it in profit-producing team building, and how to use associated techniques to enhance your own and your team's effectiveness and competitive capabilities, you will be impressed! So will the people you work for.

Identifying Your Own Strengths and Weaknesses

Begin your own self-discovery process. Read the work of leading management theorists and articulate discussions by reputable commentators (so easy on the Internet!), and check out the current literature on the subject. But you will need something even more critical: feedback on how effective you are as a manager or team leader. How can you become more effective if you don't get some straight talk on how you are being perceived by relevant others?

Getting feedback is always a humbling experience, and sometimes that can be scary. It can raise all kinds of insecurities. *Suppose I'm not good enough? Suppose I have some deep character flaws? Suppose I won't be able to be as successful as I want to be?*

Feedback about personal behavior, style, mannerisms, and reactions regarding how you come across to others must be presented in a positive and constructive context. Otherwise, you won't accept the feedback, just like people disregard or react angrily to harsh criticism. A number of consulting firms have come up with tools for providing feedback, and similar information can be obtained from university-based and commercial career centers.

You can make a start on your own by filling out the simple questionnaire on the next page. If your responses to this simple self-assessment reveal one or more weaknesses, you will know where to begin on your developmental path. If you don't have a weakness or two, you're probably not being honest with yourself. This will be a problem if you are a team builder or team leader.

The *Managerial Assessment of Proficiencies* and many other programs use this kind of feedback device to help people focus on their relative strengths in specific, team-building competencies. Since these competencies were identified by researchers surveying many thousands of successful managers, this kind of specific feedback represents a set of conceptual stepping stones toward success as a team leader.

A Short Self-Assessment

Circle your response to each of the questions below. Be as honest as you can.

I am a patient person.

Yes   **Usually**   **A Weakness**

Others think I am easy to approach.

Yes   **Usually**   **A Weakness**

I never feel that I am superior in some ways to my co-workers.

Yes   **Usually**   **A Weakness**

I really get a kick out of making other people look good.

Yes   **Usually**   **A Weakness**

It's not in my nature to be punishing in my comments.

Yes   **Usually**   **A Weakness**

I never fail to thank people for work done well.

Yes   **Usually**   **A Weakness**

I am frequently acknowledged for my contributions to others' successes.

Yes   **Usually**   **A Weakness**

I feel good about having opportunities to coach others.

Yes   **Usually**   **A Weakness**

I have no hesitation about telling people when their work is not okay.

Yes   **Usually**   **A Weakness**

If people can't perform, I have no problem with firing them.

Yes   **Usually**   **A Weakness**

A Closer Look at Competencies

We will take a close look at three managerial competencies in this chapter: *Appraising People and Performance, Training, Coaching, and Delegating; and Disciplining and Counseling.*

But the more immediate task is to define with some precision exactly what competences are and why they're important.

Our use of the term "competency" refers to what one needs to know in order to perform satisfactorily, and the characteristics that are required for successful performance.

"Competency" can be said to refer to ability of perform a task against a standard. Assessment of performance against standards determines whether or not specific competences are present.

"Competency" also refers to:

- Any of several complementary sets of knowledge, abilities, skills, and characteristics that enable an individual to perform specified tasks in a satisfactory manner.

- A prerequisite set of skills necessary for getting the job.

A "competency model" is a stated set of competencies required to be successful in a job. It should be tailored to the requirements of the current job and those of the evolving organization (how jobs are likely to change in the near future). Performance gaps can be identified and closed, and the organization's goals for professional and personal growth can be defined for all employees, from executives on down to new hires.

Finally, a competency model provides a framework for enhancing corporate performance by turning employees into the corporation's "secret weapon." Technologies can be duplicated, but not the performance and commitment of competency-rich teams.

One senior manager I once spoke with said this about training: "I send you a few people because they really need to learn. I send a somewhat larger group as a reward for good work. But I send most with the hope that you can get through to them so I don't have to fire them." These days, short-duration, in-house training focuses on competencies that can be used to close performance gaps efficiently and at minimal cost.

The Massachusetts Institute of Technology Office of Careers defines competencies as characteristics (i.e. skills, knowledge, self-concept, traits, and motives) that enable us to be successful in our interactions with others at work, school, home, and in our community at large.

I believe the sets of competencies required for team building are pretty straightforward:

1. Appraising people and performance
2. Training, coaching, and delegating
3. Disciplining and counseling

What knowledge, skills, and abilities are involved? And what is it that a team leader has to know and do? Let's take these three competencies from the top.

Appraising People and Performance

Our performance is always being observed and appraised. It's an unavoidable part of the human condition. But ideally, it should be ranked according to performance against standards, since that creates a close approximation of equal opportunity. Other performance factors that should be considered include general contributions to the team, ability to relate to others, cooperation, initiative, and support of others.

Many organizations are concerned about fairness and bias; some people believe that it's wrong to rank people. But if you consider the performance-related attributes listed above (each of which can be considered a sub-competence), a good argument can be made in defense of assigned rankings. Organizational survival depends upon continuous renewal, which can only happen when there is continuous performance improvement through skill-building and assessment, replacement of weak performers with competent individuals, and broadening the base of competent performers.

In the world of sports, some people take the field and some sit on the bench. The employees that the company values the most tend to get the most training and other benefits, and everyone knows who they are—which people are the "norm-busters," the ones who are consistently the first to finish tasks, and the ones who take the time to help others.

It's still necessary to keep accurate performance records and anecdotal reports on every employee, however.

Appraising performance is relatively easy if you have performance standards and a reasonably unambiguous task structure. For every task or piece of work, there has to be a way to define "okay" and "not okay." When work is okay, you need to say *Thanks!* When it's not okay, you need to sit down with the worker involved to find out what happened. Never tolerate a mistake.

Your first task in performance appraisal is to make sure there are performance standards for all work, and that everyone on the team knows the standards and accepts them as fair.

Appraising performance requires…

Knowledge about:

- Appraisal as a process
- Standards and how to establish or find them
- Performance measurements
- Corporate requirements

Ability to:

- Collect and assess performance information
- Follow corporate assessment guidelines
- Use corporate documentation formats and forms

Skill in:

- Communicating performance data in a positive manner
- Using performance data as a basis for setting improvement tactics

Other characteristics:

- Experience in talking about performance and guiding others
- Sensitivity to anxiety in those being assessed

Pay attention. If there is a single, bedrock skill that team builders need to master, it is performance assessment. It gives you the metrics needed to benchmark an individual's performance, and thereby creates the "ground" from which you begin to help them achieve higher performance levels.

> Assessment will shape your positive relationship with team members if they see you as fair, objective, constructive, and helpful in assessing their performance.

Training, Coaching, and Delegating

Training, coaching, and *delegating* are directly involved in the quest for better, faster, cheaper performance. In fact, improved performance is virtually impossible if team leaders and managers are not competent in all these areas. Develop yourself and you will have a better idea of how to prepare employees to do what will be needed to reach new market opportunities and keep their jobs from being outsourced.

Let me be as explicit as I can: You must be competent in these three areas if you are going to be able to help a team perform successfully and extend performance capabilities. That means setting targets or other measurable increments to move from current performance to a new, higher level (i.e., to "produce three more units per day" or to "reduce re-work by five percent in the next month").

Training needs were probably best defined many years ago by Leonard Nadler, considered by many to be the "father" of human resource development.[1] Nadler created a simple training-needs model that is based on desired level of performance. Subtract from that the performance you're getting now, and what you get is the performance "gap" that needs to be closed. The next steps in his model describe how to structure and implement developmental experiences.

Simple enough, but first you need to know exactly what level of performance is needed (and that's not always easy to define). Then you must be able to accurately assess performance. If you do not have the standards to do that, this seemingly easy subtraction process probably will require some time and a lot of thought. However, one shortcut is to prove the value of participation by asking the people who already meet or exceed needed performance levels this question: What do others need to know and what do they need to know how to do to be able to perform at your level? Admittedly, it would be easier if the deficit were in inches or pounds, but do consider this: If you can't measure it, you can't criticize, critique, or correct it.

Team leaders need to keep a close watch on the performance of each team member and look for bits and pieces of performance that can be improved through short-interval training. Beyond improving performance, it is imperative to continue performance improvement. Even the incredible golfer Tiger Woods has a coach for his swing (and maybe for putting, too).

Effective training requires…

Knowledge about:
- Defining performance gaps
- Prescribing short-interval remedial training
- Training resources that can help you close performance gaps
- Adult learning theory and curriculum design (how to develop and lay out learning modules)

Ability to:
- Discuss performance deficits in a supportive manner
- Define and present short-interval training that is required

- Propose ways for individuals to receive necessary training
- Provide personal assistance

Skill in:

- Defining *specific* training needs
- Getting agreement from individuals whose performance requires remedial support

Also necessary if you want to be effective at training:

- Experience in assisting others with performance-improving coaching and training
- An ability to encourage and be supportive
- An understanding regarding how to use yourself as a trainer

Training that is paid for by the company is supposed to be an investment in individuals, for the benefit of the company. However, the more time the training takes and the more people it involves, the less likely the company will ever benefit fully or substantially from its investment. (This is a major reason why many potentially valuable training programs or methods fall out of favor.)

Short-interval training translates as hours, not days. Using Nadler's suggested approach to defining training needs, it should be possible to come up with very specific performance gaps. The more specific the definition of the gap, the less time required to close it. (Keep in mind that training that can be done in *hours* is more likely to be authorized and funded.)

Coaching is about fine-tuning individual performance by making minor corrections and suggestions and providing team members with insights and observations regarding elements of their individual and collective performance. This should happen as soon as possible after the actual performance so the details being discussed are still fresh in the minds of the team leader and team members.

Coaching should not be confused with close supervision or looking over someone's shoulder, and it is not the same thing as controlling. Football coaches, basketball coaches, and baseball coaches are not role models for the kind of coaching being described here. (In truth, athletic coaches tend to be authoritarian, and they certainly make decisions about who sits on the bench and whose performance no longer qualifies them for the team.)

Think of an individual who gets down on one knee next to a desk to make suggestions or offer words of encouragement, or someone at lunch who says something like, "The next time you make a presentation like the one this morning, you might want to distribute the handouts *after* the presentation so people pay attention to what you're saying instead of reading ahead."

Informal coaching is specific, brief, and based on an actual observation. It is without right/wrong judgments—just a small suggestion from one professional to another. If it comes from a team leader, it's not a suggestion that team members are likely to ignore.

Successful coaching requires…

Knowledge about:
- Coaching as a proactive team-building method
- Recent and past performance of team members

Ability to:

- Provide often disconfirming information without invoking anger or resentment
- Offer help, not criticism (publicly and privately)

Skill in:

- Building "helping" relationships with team members
- Identifying those times when coaching is needed and how to meet the specific need
- Maintaining a positive and encouraging tone, regardless of the issue being discussed

Other characteristics:

- A high degree of interpersonal skill
- Personal discipline to consistently follow up after every coaching moment to correct or reinforce performance

A recurring image for me is the famous photograph of a police officer bending over to talk to a small child. It carried the message "A man never stands so tall as when he stoops to help a child." Coaching is about small corrections, nudges in the right direction, a few quiet words. It can also take the form of a sit-down conversation where you replay in detail something a team member did, and comment about other options that could be tried next time. This is what happens when a football team sits down to look at game films: to analyze missed blocks, dropped passes, etc.

Coaching is another way to contribute to the success of team members.

Delegating is a major weakness among team leaders. Many managers say that it's more trouble than it's worth—that it's easier to do something themselves than to give it to someone else. There is some truth in each of these statements, but in the context of *team building*, delegating is essential. You must give people "success" experiences and opportunities that allow them to stretch themselves and grow, as well as to become committed to each other and a common purpose. Delegation is a necessary part of this learning and socializing process.

When you are developing a team, remember that each team member needs to learn about every role in greater detail and better understand the organizational setting in which they work. They can do this if you delegate tasks that are not normally part of their daily work. This "stretches" people and forces them to learn things that are outside their comfort zone. Otherwise, how can you evaluate talent, flexibility, and willingness to learn?

Delegation is a way of testing what has been learned and checking to be sure that new behaviors are being applied.

Successful delegating requires…

Knowledge about:
- Delegation as a development tool
- Supervising work that has been delegated
- Building on skills acquired through delegation in order to strengthen individual and team performance

Ability to:
- Determine appropriate delegation opportunities
- Ensure the success of individuals performing delegated tasks

- Keep individuals moving toward higher levels of performance

Skill in:

- Providing encouragement to accept challenges
- Celebrating successes
- Convincing all team members to keep growing

Other characteristics:

- Willingness to take a chance on people and to spread ability and competence throughout the team (rather than holding on to high-visibility roles
- Personal commitment to develop team members

Delegation is a way to shape behavior on an ongoing basis.

Disciplining and Counseling

It's unfortunate that disciplining and counseling carry negative connotations. True, they come into play when an employee's performance does not meet accepted standards, but they are both necessary competencies, since most organizations require them ("Three strikes and you're out!" or "You have to spend 10 days in the penalty box"—that kind of thing). State and federal laws establish fair-employment rules that protect employees against discrimination and unfair personnel actions, which only reinforces the need for team leaders and managers to understand these two competencies in detail.

People fire themselves! Most adults manage to negotiate their private lives without behavior or performance problems. Why should they have such problems at work? Actually, there are many reasons why performance is poor. Some people are generally unhappy about life. Others have real or imagined impediments to their success. Some people really are not competent to perform assigned tasks, or they hate their manager and some or all of their co-workers. What's to fix? Help these people with their résumés, direct them to another organization where they might be happier, and say goodbye.

All these possibilities present a compelling argument as to why you should NOT provide much performance help during an employee's probationary period, beyond giving new employees a complete orientation.

Savvy HR managers and hiring managers will not allow anyone whose performance is doubtful to remain past the last day of probation. Why hire someone permanently who will be a problem employee? Because they need the job? (Are you a social worker?)

When it comes to *disciplining,* be sure you and all your employees understand your organization's formal process. There are three main disciplinary steps used in most organizations: (1) a verbal reprimand that is documented; (2) a written warning; and (3) termination. Check with your HR department for more details on this particularly important issue.

Be clear about the difference between *disciplining* and *counseling. Disciplining* is about getting compliance—about getting people to "shape up," conform to the organization's norms, and perform well enough to meet the standards for their assigned tasks. *Counseling* is about helping people whose performance is marginal (but whose other behaviors are okay) to map out plans for their own growth, development, and survival in the organization. The manager or team leader is not paid to punish people. In too many workplaces, a "counseling session" is understood to be a punitive process— a remedial action that follows unsuccessful performance or other unacceptable behavior. In fact, it's really a last attempt to keep someone on staff, so it is a positive process.

Performance counseling is a good way to make sure that people understand the organization's performance requirements and know that they are expected to meet them. When individuals fail to make appropriate behavioral choices, the manager or team leader has a responsibility to do two things: remind them one last time of their obligations to the company, and give them an opportunity to make different choices. This is done only after prior coaching, warnings, and offers of help. If they choose not to comply, then the manager has to make a decision as to what is best for the company.

Get Rid of Non-Performers

Everyone must understand that the problem is serious, which is why a formal meeting is held to put an individual on notice that he or she is in danger of termination. Documentation is necessary: There should be a written description of the imperfect or inadequate performance (with specifics), and the employee must be notified verbally and in writing that he or she is on a downhill slide out of the organization.

When there is a persistent performance problem that has not been resolved despite multiple attempts at coaching, a formal meeting should be convened with the team leader and the team member. Supporting documentation should be prepared in advance to lay out the case against the individual, but also to give the team leader an opportunity to assess all prior efforts to help the individual succeed in the job and in the organization.

The team leader begins by discussing the employee's performance and apparent inability to accept coaching guidance, explaining that this is becoming an impediment to the performance of the team. The team leader explains clearly that if another formal meeting is necessary, the consequences might be termination if the individual fails to bring his or her performance up to the required standard, using the remedial practices suggested.

The manager and the employee should then agree on a plan to change the behavior satisfactorily, with close managerial oversight. A follow-up meeting should be scheduled at this time to see that everything's back to *fully* satisfactory performance. (This follow-up meeting is also another chance for the boss to give one more "Don't screw up again!" pep talk.)

This is the formal route, when the first termination document is being developed after one or more verbal warnings have gone unheeded and the performance counseling meeting has been conducted. There are consequences to the team leader/manager for taking this route if the team member involved is popular, if the offenses involved are really relatively minor, if other workers think the boss is trying to prove he/she is tough, or if everyone thinks the boss is out of line.

All these factors suggest that it's better to try to handle things informally—one more reason why you should put together a team of people who know and respect each other and share a common set of objectives. They will be able to work out the problems within the team (another team member, for example, is quite likely to confront the nonconforming member and provide the necessary warning). That might be the best way to do it, anyway.

The goal here always is to get optimum output. Being legalistic and punitive is not the way to get it: it's far better to use informal channels. Cutting out a team member saps the team's energy (unless, of course, the individual involved is really a rotten performer or a troublemaker and is generally disliked).

Suppose Fred is having a second "off" day. The team leader has a choice: Confront Fred ("Hey, Fred. What's the matter?") or ask another team member to do it ("Jim, could you check with Fred? He seems to be having another off day").

This accomplishes two things. First, it keeps the responsibility to deal with Fred at an informal level. Second, it tells Jim and others who notice or find out (and most will) that Fred is also their responsibility, because his non-performance is impacting group productivity.

But suppose Fred's not a guy any of the other team members care about? Then the manager or team leader has to act. (Remember: What you tolerate, you validate!)

Effective disciplining requires…

Knowledge about:

- Corporate policy regarding non-performing employees
- Procedures to be followed and forms or documentation to be used
- Financial and other costs associated with losing an employee

Ability to:

- Conduct a formal counseling session
- Talk about possible job loss without being threatening or punitive
- Keep the possibility of successful recovery alive throughout the conversation

Skill in:

- Providing disconfirming feedback in a gentle, fact-based manner
- Being supportive while being firm

Other characteristics:

- An understanding that removing people is part of the job
- A commitment to maintain standards

It seems anachronistic to be talking about things such as getting rid of people, confronting non-performance, and finding out why people don't perform. It's the complete antithesis of developing teams for competent performance, mutual support, growth, and the achievement of corporate goals. Nevertheless, actions of last resort need to be identified, and this one has been.

Chapter 7 Note

1. Leonard Nadler is widely credited with coining the term "human resource development." His first book, *Human Resource Development* (1970), is considered a classic in the field of training and development. Throughout the 1970s and 1980s, Nadler tirelessly advocated for the HRD profession. He has written a number of books on the subject for various publishers, including *Designing Training Programs: The Critical Events Model* (Butterworth Heineman, 2nd edition, 1994) and *The Handbook of Human Resource Development.* He is professor emeritus at George Washington University.

    If you are serious about training as a profession or are interested in team building, become familiar with his work.

Chapter 8

Are Teams Counter-Cultural?

An interesting insight into teams appears in an entry listed in Wikipedia, an online encyclopedia that presents information contributed by the public. The individual who contributed it wrote that for thousands of years, people had time to ease into relationships. Now, almost everyone at work is expected to instantly slip in and out of multiple team roles. There's no "book" on how to do that, however. Perhaps thousands of years of evolution frustrate our ability to perform effectively in quickly formed teams, and the best we can do is start focusing on job roles.

The team leader can decide on the purpose of the team, the tasks to be accomplished, and the reason each role representative is involved, but from that point on, how quickly the team gels and achieves its mission will depend on the extent to which members know how to fill these task and maintenance roles:

Task Functions

- *Initiating:* Proposing ideas that launch or maintain discussion.
- *Information- or opinion-seeking:* Asking for supporting information.
- *Information- or opinion-giving:* Providing input.
- *Clarifying or elaborating:* Interpreting ideas, giving examples.

- *Summarizing:* Pulling comments together, offering a conclusion.
- *Consensus testing:* Checking for agreement.

Maintenance Functions

- *Encouraging:* Being complimentary, giving recognition to others.
- *Expressing group feelings:* Sensing and expressing the mood of the group.
- *Harmonizing:* Smoothing-over, reconciling disagreements.
- *Compromising:* Looking for a middle ground to resolve conflict.
- *Gate-keeping:* Bringing silent members into the discussion.
- *Setting standards:* Asking "Is this the best we can do?"

Hindering Functions

- *Dominating:* Appearing authoritative, over-communicating.
- *Withdrawing:* Becoming non-participative.
- *Degrading:* Making disrespectful or discouraging comments.
- *Not cooperating:* Blocking, using hidden agendas to frustrate progress.
- *Engaging in side conversations:* Private chatter, giggling, not paying attention.

Note: The fact that this list has appeared twice in this small book says that it's important. Pay attention.

> The motivational power that drives teamwork comes from interpersonal skills, rather than from task structure or authority.

Remember the discussion back in Sociology 101 about roles and role-playing? We are, concurrently, a son or daughter, spouse, parent, manager, employee, co-worker, friend, acquaintance, neighbor, member of professional associations and religious groups, shopper, consumer, and so on.

Each role requires us to make shifts in our behavior and our responses. We do this many times a day every day, and usually smoothly and without thought. So what's so special about being a team member at work? Why should it be difficult, different, or challenging? Try these reasons: Responsibility. Visibility. Vulnerability.

In the traditional workplace, workers can be pretty anonymous. They come on time, leave with other people, call no attention to themselves, are polite when spoken to, and make no demands on others. Color them gray.

By contrast, everyone on a well-developed team knows one another: their strengths, their weaknesses, their preferences, their work history, and an amazing array of personal details. Each team is a full complement of competencies, and the members are in the process of developing an even stronger package of knowledge, skills, and abilities. Each member of the team has specific tasks to perform (responsibilities) at a satisfactory level or better. If they fail at this, everyone on the team will know (visibility) and there will be no excuses and no way to avoid culpability (vulnerability). In most work situations, there are many ways to fix or hide screw-ups, and generally a lot of time to do it. Not so in a high-performance team.

Kinds of Teams

Most fans never stop to think that sports teams are among the most authoritarian organizations around. Performance is the only thing that matters. That makes sports teams the ultimate equal opportunity environment: Competent performance gets you in, but when someone can perform your role better, you're gone! Few people want to work in such demanding and unforgiving environments, with the possible exception of star athletes.

In many project teams, each individual is expected to contribute to the project, working at their normal work stations and doing work for the project as a collateral duty. (Think matrix organization.) Members of such project teams have to attend some project meetings, but in other project teams, the managers attend meetings and assign the work to their direct reports. Not much team building there.

Then there's the "vertical" project organization, in which a project manager is responsible for the budget, the schedule, and all necessary resources for the duration of the project. Team building makes sense here.

There are also teams set up to design new systems or protocols or develop new procedures for specific purposes. Volunteer organizations, non-governmental organizations, churches, and civic groups all have projects and teams. Some of them must accept anyone who wants to participate, while others can be highly selective. The usual circumstance is that one individual is designated a team leader and is told to take the available workers and turn them into a team. Not an ideal situation, but it is the path to promotion for those who succeed as team leaders.

How to Build a High-Performance Team

If there is such a thing as an ideal team-building opportunity or situation, it's one in which you are able to use demanding criteria to choose team members from groups of highly-qualified candidates.

Gretchen Chartier of Koch Financial Services in Phoenix has more than 20 years' experience working with start-up companies. Koch Financial is her third. She described the kinds of people you search out to start a company that can "do money" successfully.

"The perfect team consists of people who are acknowledged experts in their fields. Their reputations are a major selling point for the company. You need a 'scholar' type who brings a research-based aura to the team; an 'entrepreneurial' type who has a track record in building businesses; a 'money' type who is deeply experienced in making money work; and an 'administrator' type who is the office manager and executive assistant—an expeditor who can get things done quickly and always with the company's image in mind."

According to Chartier, all must have "Type A" personalities; they must be people who are driven to achieve and who are addicted to a workaholic lifestyle. Further, they need to be passionate about what they're doing, tireless in task accomplishment, and driven by a "can-do" attitude. They must also possess an over-the-top sense of enthusiasm for the success of the company. Underlying all this should be a well-honed survival instinct that keeps a start-up going and profitable.

Chartier offers some very direct and unambiguous suggestions for team leaders:

Rules for Team Leaders	
Rule #1:	Always hire people who are smarter than you are.
Rule #2:	Make sure you know and understand the job of each team manager.
Rule #3:	DO NOT micro-manage. If you need to do that, work someplace else.
Rule #4:	Do not become a "friend." Be a mentor and a sounding board.
Rule #5:	Follow the corporate rules.
Rule #6:	Praise good work.
Rule #7:	Discuss poor work.

Ms. Chartier's comments are echoed by Bernard Moon, founder of many IT-related companies, most currently GoingOn Networks, Inc.[1] When it comes to selecting people for a start-up, he advises this: "Never settle when it comes to personnel. One A-grade hire equals ten C-grade hires." Since A-quality people tend to attract other A-quality people, he asks these questions about potential hires:

Do they get things done?
What is their track record?
Can they deal with risk?

How much risk are they willing to take?
What is their growth potential?
Are they constantly seeking to improve themselves?

Further confirmation comes from southern California consultant and graduate school professor Ichok Adizer, who said that a team needs the following kinds of people:

Producer: This kind of person knows how to get the job done.

Administrator: This kind of person is able to plan and organize.

Entrepreneur: This kind of person has vision and creative problem-solving skills.

Integrator: This kind of person can take an individual goal and transform it into a group goal.[2]

These various prescriptions for successful team building are representative of the high end of the continuum, but they speak clearly to the kinds of personal and intellectual attributes that leaders should be looking for when putting together a high-performance team.

> A high-performance team is always a counter-cultural phenomenon.

Members of high-performance teams are different from other workers. If "satisfactory performance" is the norm and is the basic requirement for continuing as an employee of an organization, then it follows that "high performance" must be several cuts above satisfactory, and that members of high-performance teams must also be "better than" ordinary employees. Such distinctions are hard to discuss in the best of settings, because they can be construed as a kind of caste that is separate from managers and workers. This presents a challenge to corporate egalitarianism, so think very carefully about how you can encourage your high-performing team without discouraging or dismissing everybody else. They are also doing important work!

Chapter 8 Notes

1. Bernard Moon, quoted in "Building the Perfect Team" (www.alwayson-network.com, August 30, 2005).

2. Ichok Adizer, quoted in "Team Building for Change Management" (http://www.managingchange.biz/change_management_team_buildi ng.html).

Chapter 9

Not All Teams Are Worth the Name

It's easier to achieve success with purpose-driven teams such as start-ups and high-profile project teams where you select the team than it is with teams that are organized around ongoing work. In the examples of start-up companies cited in Chapter 8, earning big money was the purpose. The ability to contribute to such enterprises is the established high bar for admission to become a member of the team. That makes sense, and so do the admission criteria.

Some Teams Can be Helped, and Some Can't

Two different kinds of teams benefit most from team-building activities. First come the teams that are already very good and secure in their roles, but want to get better in order to make more money for themselves and the company.

The second type of team in which people will really work together is one in which every job is on the line. With such teams, everyone is motivated and purpose-driven. The company involved in the following true story is now out of business, so it will not be a violation to share this important lesson about an 11-man team that was only weeks away from being fired. Here's the story:

A True Story About Teamwork

The scene: A Wednesday-to-Saturday retreat for the 11 senior managers of a manufacturing plant.

The reason for the retreat: A union vote is going to be held in six weeks. The plant will probably be organized. The 11 men at the retreat were trained to work together for a year while the plant was under construction. They were given three success criteria: Production date, profit date, no unions. Fail at any of them, and the entire team will be replaced. Production and profit dates have been met, but their plant is about to be unionized. Therefore, their jobs are on the line.

The retreat began with cocktails and dinner. A lot of nervous chatter. After dinner, a movie and discussion of teams, team work, and team building. Then, an exercise:

The consultant had drawn a circle on the flipchart and listed all 11 names around the circle. His instructions: "Gentlemen, here are three markers. Black will represent positive "I like you and work well with you" relationships. Blue will represent cool, distant, not quite trustful relationships. Red will represent relationships characterized by distrust and dislike. Use the markers to draw lines that describe your relationships from your name to each of the other 10 names."

The consultant then withdrew, leaving all eleven managers with 15 minutes of agonizing silence. Finally, the plant manager said, "I guess I have to be the first," so he went to the flipchart and began to draw lines from his name to the others. There were 5 reds, 4 blacks, and 2 blues.

The other managers followed. All drew some red lines, but blue was the predominant color. Sometimes the lines were the same color in both directions. Some members of the team were surprised to get red lines, but everyone got at least one red line. No one got all red lines.

The process took more than an hour. When the consultant returned, he said, "This picture you've drawn is a sociogram, a picture of how you work together. The problems you have in the plant probably are related to these relationship patterns. The sociogram will remain taped to the wall so you can study it. Before we leave at noon on Saturday, I want to be able to put in the plant manager's hand a contract signed by the people on both ends of every red line that states:

- What the problem is between you.
- What you are going to do about it.
- What help you will need, and from whom.
- How someone else will know that the problem has been solved.

"Breakfast is at 7:30 a.m. I will see you at 8:30 a.m."

There were no conversations as the 11 men left the room.

Thursday and Friday were devoted to more films, input from the consultant, exercises, and small-group work. No one worked on their contracts.

The Friday evening cocktail hour went longer than planned. Dinner was a somber occasion. Then, when they walked into the room to set up for the evening work session, they all took notice of another flipchart circle with their names around the perimeter.

"This time," the consultant said, "there will be no blue marker. This time, just black and red. Black for 'I trust you, I support you, and I expect the same from you.' Or red for 'I don't trust you because you don't support me.'" Again, the line-drawing took an hour. Many of the blue lines had turned into red lines.

The consultant handed out a few contract forms for them to see, and left a stack of them at the front of the room. He said, "I will be here to help if any of you want to involve me." No one did, but they worked until four in the morning to complete the process.

At 8:30 Saturday morning, the consultant put the contracts on the table in front of the plant manager. "My job is done," he said to the team. "Your jobs have just begun, because you have to go back to the plant on Monday and deal with the threats to your jobs.

"Just so you know, I was told that even some of your supervisors have been telling the workers to vote for the union. One said, 'For God's sake! Get a union in here. When work doesn't get done, everyone gets blamed. I'm sick of this stuff! If I could vote for the union, I would do it!' Maybe as a closing exercise, you should share with each other what you learned."

Again, the consultant withdrew and let the 11 participants share their testimonials, their apologies, and their commitments to the team and to their mutual survival. They undoubtedly understood that it was their failure to cooperate and to be mutually supportive that caused the problem down on the plant floor—that it was their own egos and game-playing that had been their undoing.

It needs to be mentioned again that all 11 men had trained together for a year—training in finance and management, taking field trips to other plants, and participating in several week-long episodes of experiential learning and team-building in which honesty, trust, and sharing were the big lessons. You would think that after a year of being trained to work as a team that they would have been able to overcome the cultural baggage that each person brought to the job, but they couldn't.

This all took place several years ago, but if you put these same people together now (any one of whom you would be pleased to have as a next-door neighbor), I believe that the "cultural imperative" to play win-lose games would surface again and override everything they've learned about teams, team building, and team work. These days we call it "baggage," the stuff we bring with us from one life episode to another that gets in the way. In personal relationships, it might be kids, debts, or an intrusive former spouse. In work relationships, it might be antagonism toward management, mistrust of all supervisors, and a misguided belief in the "me-first, the hell with the rest" ethos. The current wave of mistrust of corporations that have down-sized and outsourced away their credibility with workers (and managers, too, most of whom keep their résumés close at hand), has produced a lot of baggage.

What can team builders do? Be mindful that such regressive energies might be afoot in your team. Ask team members to stay in the present and to restrain themselves from poisoning the well from which they all must drink. In reality, though, these things are easier said than done.

That team-building exercise was highly successful. The management team, with the help of internal HR staff members, was able to convince most employees to vote against the union, though the vote was close. However, in other consulting situations, the exercise didn't work. Why?

In one situation, a team of 15 men (again, no women) was many months late and many millions of dollars over budget on the design of a product. The prototypes had been accepted by a major international corporation that was waiting to buy all the product the company could produce. The participants in the retreat were "blame-gaming" each other, and a serious exercise like the one just described seemed appropriate. When they saw the circle with their names on it, however, the 15 participants just sat and looked at it. The project manager left to smoke a cigarette.

"What's going on?" I asked him.

"You guys don't understand," he said. "This is a small community, and everyone feels lucky to live here. It's a really great place to live. I guarantee you, no one is going to make a mark on that flipchart!" If the project manager said not one person would touch the flipchart, you could take it to the bank.

"What about the project? The client? The money the company has invested?" I asked.

"They'll get over it," the project manager said. He and the other team members knew that their company and their neighbors wouldn't let them down.

A leader of another team where there was obvious intra-team conflict said to me, "They're not going to fire us. We'd be too hard to replace. So let's just have some fun and games and call it a day."

I remember another team-building experience, this with a group of 12 men and women, the top R & D professionals in a major pharmaceutical company, who absolutely refused to work together to prepare a report for their corporate VP. They had the information and the task was clear and appropriate, but they had other agendas, one of which apparently was to make their boss look bad.

These failures of logic in favor of personal and collective agendas are mentioned to make the point that success or failure to build a team will depend on forces other than the team leader's energy and commitment; history, baggage, and old resentments can frustrate the most enthusiastic team builder, and when that seems to be the case, some team leaders find it more constructive to manage an unresponsive work group by using high structure, short-interval targets and deadlines in order to get compliance and performance. Sometimes, however, the culture of a group cannot be bent to team building; trying to do something counter-cultural would be like trying to make water run uphill. Neither can happen without a lot of force, and that pretty well invalidates all the reasons for having a team.

> Building teams and corralling social pressure to get people to conform to demands for perform- ance is the new alternative to authority.

Authority never worked that well anyway, and in these politically correct times, it is never going to sell.

Context and Team Building

Outsourcing makes a lot of sense in many, many situations.

Now, think back to the team-building competencies discussed earlier. I suggest that there's a connection between getting serious about firing people for non-performance and building high-performance teams. Consequences are a necessary element in shaping and maintaining socially acceptable behavior. But consequences alone are not sufficient.

In the unusually titled book *Getting Yours,* Thomas K. Connellan described how he once offered to work on a double-or-nothing basis to change the behavior of any group of employees. He guaranteed that he would be able to meet agreed-upon change targets. His method was behavior modification: antecedent, behavior, consequences (ABC). Well, yes, there were some conditions. Three of them: He would have to be given the freedom to change compensation levels; the freedom to make on-the-spot cash awards; and the freedom to fire anyone who didn't go along with his program.

Back then, there weren't many workplaces where a consultant could get access to those kinds of freedoms. It's probably impossible these days.

But the ABC idea is neat. Essentially, you do some things to set people up to behave in certain ways. That's actually okay—it's what team leaders are supposed to do. Then, you watch them behave. If they get it right, there's a reward.

But suppose they get it wrong? Unhappy consequences. A penalty.

Rewards are good, penalties are bad. Most team leaders do not like that part of the job, nor do most people. This brings us to what team leaders need to do to solve problems. The late Gordon Lippitt developed an all-purpose problem-solving model, which he presented to the Annual Conference of Friends (Quakers) in Philadelphia in 1966.[2] It looks like this:

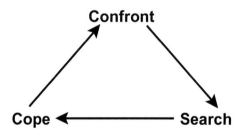

The message here is so simple and obvious that it has become a universal problem-solving methodology.

The first thing you have to do is to admit the fact that there is a problem, and confront it. Nothing constructive can happen until someone says, "Hey guys, we've got a problem!"

Once the problem is acknowledged, then and only then can people do something about the problem. What can be done? You have to initiate a search process to find a constructive way to respond. In any situation, the first fix will probably be somewhat tentative, but the search process will produce a response everyone can live with, for a while at least.

If the fix doesn't take, everyone is going to have to make adjustments to cope with the imperfect solution, but it won't be long before coping becomes an energy drain and tries everyone's patience. So, what to do? Confront the fact that you've still got a problem. Then go through the three-step cycle again.

This simple model works. The only thing it requires is for someone to have the coverage to admit that there's a problem and that something has to be done about it. The team leader is generally the only one who can make the call. If that's the case, don't let the team wallow too long in a situation that cannot have a positive outcome. Intervene. Stop the wallowing, the wasted time, the wasted effort, the wasted energy, the disappointment in the team leader. Stop the pain and provide relief! ("Hey, guys, we've got a problem.") Then begin the search for solutions. People who were silent before might have some constructive suggestions.

It is important that the team grow from the experience. After the problem has been solved, the team leader should say something like this: "I'm not the only one who knew we were blocked and getting nowhere. Why didn't any of you call it? Maybe that's your responsibility, too, as an effective team member."

Chapter 9 Notes

1. Thomas K. Connellan, 1982. *Getting Yours: Success Strategies for the 1980s.* Secaucas, New York: Lyle Stuart.

2. Gordon Lippitt was a professor at George Washington University in D.C., a frequent author and collaborator, an early advocate of organization development, and a founder of the National Training Institutes (through which sensitivity training was developed into a now-neglected managerial training tool). Perhaps his most popular book was *Organization Renewal: A Holistic Approach to Organization Development,* which he wrote in 1981.

Chapter 10

Getting Down to the Nitty-Gritty

You can learn a lot about team building simply by visiting consultants' web sites. Purveyors of team skills will tell you right off what they will do for you, your team, and your company. As you consider such information, ask yourself this: *With our people, what would be the half-life of this kind of experience? Do we have the leaders to sustain the follow-up effort required to maintain team training? Would we be able to get our money's worth in added value? Or would team building just be entertainment?*

There are at least three major benefits to working on team building:

- Teams will maximize your organization's human resources through the magic multiplier: synergy.

- Committed teams generally outperform individuals, thus giving you superior output and results.

- Improvement is continuous, as team successes beget more success and more confidence among people who are willing to show others what they can do.

It only takes to or three days to become somewhat familiar with the team-building competencies: training, coaching, and delegating; appraising people and performance; and disciplining and counseling. When you have internalized the competencies and the values they are based on, you will demonstrate this through your actions. It's possible that you can learn to apply these competencies on your own, but it is far better to practice your new behaviors within a supportive group or a group that you want to shape into a team. The point is to get fast feedback on the consequences of your actions—the things that work and those that don't.

Pushing toward the end of this guide, let's look at a team's life cycle and consider key roles team builders and team leaders need to play throughout start-up, maintenance, and disbanding.

Forming, Maintaining, and Disbanding a Team

Forming a Team

Here are my best recommendations for this critical first stage:

1. Make certain you know what business you're going to be in. What does your manager expect in terms of results, profits, throughput, and pay-offs? In project management terms, what's your charter? To whom do you report? What are your prerogatives? What are the limits of your freedom to operate?

2. Decide (if you are permitted to do so) who will be on your team. Why this person or that person? What's their expertise and experience? Go to the HR office and check their records. Find out which people have been a problem for other managers, which people are marginal per- formers, and which people are effective performers. Don't prejudge too harshly, because some team members will blossom for you. But don't be blind.

3. Structure your first team meeting with precision. Use it to set the tone for the kind of operation you want, and have it reflect your personal style. When you plan your meet-

ing, answer this question: *What do I want team members to go away with?* Then prepare the materials that will give them the information you want them to have. Include the answers to item #1, above.

4. Make introductions, in case members don't know each other. Describe the role each person is expected to fill and specify the organizational areas in which the team will function or have responsibilities. Be explicit in what you say and in what you put on the handouts.

5. Tell team members where you're coming from, organizationally and operationally. Tell them how you like to work and what you expect of them. If you have a reputation, acknowledge it and provide details. This is a time to spell out ground rules.

6. If there is no mission statement, use the first meeting to get members to think about what it would be, and formulate one the second time you meet.

7. Encourage participation, but keep meetings short. Gabby meetings that run overtime set a poor example for time management. Start on time and quit on time.

8. Use the first meeting to begin to say thank you: for time and attention, for contributions, for any support that's forthcoming. Begin to communicate this message: "I will notice what you do, and will express my appreciation." This will also suggest that you will notice malfeasance and comment on it as well. Publicly.

9. Openness means that what everyone sees or knows is common property and will be discussed by the team. No

time for games. You want adult behavior and adult assumption of responsibilities.

10. If your team members do not report directly to you all the time, set up meetings with their functional managers to determine availability, and learn what commitments of time and resources they can make in support of the project. (Make sure this is in your operating charter.)

Team Maintenance

Follow these recommendations to keep a team working effectively:

1. Set targets and due dates for everything. Reduce all work to manageable increments so no one can fail. Use successes as opportunities to give out verbal rewards. If it's a big success, bring in cake and coffee or pizza and soft drinks. Pay for it yourself if there are no funds available.

2. Use delegation to stretch team members. Make them give oral reports. Require them to prepare written reports (even if they are very short). Force people to grow and to acquire more confidence.

3. When possible, have one or more team members make reports to senior management. Let them get recognition and demonstrate their competence (and your tutelage) to senior staff.

4. Never tolerate a mistake. Encourage team members to improve performance in specific areas by changing specific behaviors.

5. Use the last few minutes of every meeting to do a process check. Ask the team these questions: Is anyone unhappy? Are there issues that are being overlooked? Are you getting the support you need? Is there anyone I should contact on your behalf? Is there any information (gossip) you've heard that the rest of us need to know?

6. Use brown-bag luncheon meetings for team building and to give team members a chance to hear the ideas of guest speakers. Discuss journal articles and other professional literature. Copy articles and pass them out to team members to read on their own time. Emphasize and reward initiative, learning, and sharing.

7. Look for "plant visit" opportunities. Take your team to another work setting to observe and learn, and encourage them to bring back innovative ideas for their own team.

8. When possible, arrange for team members to participate in company-funded training programs or to represent the team at company meetings so they become more aware of the corporate context in which they are operating. Also, provide information on new bargaining contracts, and try to have copies of annual reports and other information on the company's financial standing and competitive position available for distribution.

9. Ask for volunteers to do something for the host community on weekends (i.e., become a Big Brother or Big Sister). Organize an occasional evening or Saturday event for team members and their spouses or significant others (kids, too) so team members can get to know each other socially as well as professionally. (Such activities have to

be voluntary, without penalty for those who choose not to participate or who cannot participate for other reasons.)

10. Periodically ask for feedback, but not in a self-serving way. Ask if you are meeting their expectations. If not, ask in what ways you could be doing better This will encourage team members to work on two-way communication to strengthen team performance.

11. If you are the manager-of-record and you are responsible for performance appraisals, be sure to take the process seriously. Meet with your people at least quarterly to set targets, discuss performance problems and improvements, and to express personal appreciation for efforts made on your behalf and the team. Take notes and document as much as you can; it will come in handy when you wish to nominate people for corporate recognition and rewards.

12. Be sensitive about what's going on in people's lives, and be as supportive as you can during their times of stress. When you hear that a team member has a serious personal or family problem, check with HR staff to see what kind of help is available. You might be surprised by what you and the company can do, and so will your team members.

13. Document everything you do. In particular, be sure you document targets set and met, and record details on exceptions and variances. Such records are the basis for more-accurate estimating and budgeting for future work.

14. Close collaboration with team members under the pressure of short deadlines sometimes leads to romantic relationships. Beware of the effect on other team members

and the work of the team. You might have to initiate a discussion with the people involved if personal relationships encroach.

Closing Down/Disbanding Teams

Do not dismiss the importance of this stage. Here are some helpful tips:

1. Everything has an end. Be as businesslike in shutting down a team as you were in getting started. Collect anecdotal information from team members and add it to your other documentation. It acts as your report card, your record of performance, and your basis for study and improvement regarding future team-building efforts. In the case of formal projects, keep in mind that clients usually want a shut-down report. In that case, be sure to note the positive contributions of client staff/representatives.

2. Write notes about noteworthy individual contributions for inclusion in the personnel records of team members. Such information might help them with promotions or other advantages. That good deed might even come back to you in some unexpected, beneficial way if you both remain in the same corporate structure.

3. If you have any team members who were "on loan" from a functional organization, be certain to write a note to each manager about the performance of his or her employees while they were assigned to you. This will be invaluable when those managers have to do annual performance appraisals. Do this even if it is not required. (See #2, above.)

4. If other organizational units collaborated on the project, be sure to include them in the thank-you note rituals. (See #2, above.) In these uncivil times, small acts of courtesies carry a lot of weight.

5. Make a copy of your report and send it with an appropriate cover letter to your manager of record (required or not). Include highlights of team accomplishments and note your personal learnings. Be sure to express appreciation for the assignment.

6. Take some time to write down what *you* learned. What will you do differently next time? What advice would you give a new team leader? You might be surprised by how useful this kind of written information is in team building and teamwork within the organization, and how helpful it will be in the future.

Team Building Is a Way to Extend Yourself

Do you believe in the value of each individual as a potential contributor? Do you wish your organization had a stronger ethical foundation? Are you sometimes disappointed in the personal and professional behavior of your co-workers?

Leading a team is a way to demonstrate a different way to work and perform within the organization. People will notice when a group of workers begins to perform and behave differently, reflecting pride in their work and in themselves. Such visible results matter—and they inform. When a team achieves individually and collectively in an environment of high standards, high expectations, and freely-expressed appreciation, it raises the bar for everyone else and stimulates and encourages others. Entire organizations can be changed, one team at a time.

Chapter 11

Master Your Role

Do some reading on your own to learn more about team-work and contemporary participative management. You will find a kind of religious fervor among some advocates—people get very excited when they can truly participate. There are few opportunities in life that allow us to directly and significantly influence others in such a positive way; leading a high-performance team is one of the most interesting.

Many of the big-name authors are university-based, yet bring their "better society" ideas into workplaces to prove that such ideas can actually make money for companies. Indeed, many universities have set up organizations to assist companies in team building (and no doubt are collecting research data along the way). Cornell, the University of Nebraska, Stanford, and the University of California at Berkeley all offer such help. The University of North Texas at Denton has been doing truly pioneering work on so-called "leaderless" teams. No doubt there are many more universities involved in converting theory to practice, including those schools that schedule graduate classes around the normal workday. Even NASA has its own Academy of Program and Project Leadership.

You can't be an effective team leader in any kind of organization without leaving something of yourself with the people you supervised and supported, even if only briefly. Leaders have a special responsibility to teach, to support others in personal and professional growth, and to learn along with their teams. And doing more than anyone expected can be a lot of fun.

> People who participate in a high-energy, "can-do" organization never forget it.

The U.S. is undergoing major organizational and social upheaval. The rash of buy-outs, downsizings, outsourcings, and other profit-enhancing corporate changes create whole-sale job losses and economic demotions. As a result, employees' attitudes regarding loyalty to their employer probably have been changed forever.

Organizational circumstances, too, have been changed by globalization. Sometimes, even a dedicated workforce is not enough to overcome such economic disadvantages as lower taxes, less-restrictive work rules, and labor rates that are a fraction of what workers earn in the United States and Western Europe. But maybe participation in teams can improve worker loyalty and give corporations more of a competitive edge in the race for survival.

Remember this: Companies exist to make money for shareholders, not to make specific products. Products will be dropped or added and production locations will change to support the imperative to be profitable. Globalization means job mobility. Some readers of this book will no doubt find themselves in the position of having to put together a team in a country far from home.

Social integration has never been more important. With so many people from indigenous and foreign cultures coming together in organizations around the world, it is critical to learn to work together and transcend the boundaries imposed by the cultures in which we have been reared. One colleague of mine was once involved in building a team for a major oil company that consisted of 25 individuals representing 16 nations and nine different native languages.

Years of experience with civil rights legislation and equal employment opportunity efforts in the United States convince us that large government programs alone will not overcome stereotypes and limiting ideologies. We can, however, make amazing progress in resocializing people and changing their attitudes in small groups, as long as we have opportunities to get to know one another as individuals as well as employees.

Younger employees today are of the MTV generation, accustomed to high energy, fast-paced input. The traditional organization can't offer much of that, but teams can and do. Teams can also be enormously influential in helping people move beyond the racial, gender, and religious stereotypes programmed into us. The quest for improvement becomes a reason for everyone on the team to work together and communicate more effectively, especially when building a high-performance team is the objective. Rewards and celebrations for even small successes create positive energy, which is what you need to pull people past their old barriers to discover new and satisfying working relationships.

Make performance the focus or the *raison d'etre* for people in the organization to come together, and work on building your team so that everyone can succeed, be acknowledged for their contributions, and find that synergy. When all the tips and tools in this book work for you, you will know that you are on your way to having the high-performance team you hoped for. Your co-workers will be creating positive, productive relationships with one another, and everything else will seem less important.

If anyone in corporate America is going to lead us into the future, maybe it will be the team leaders and team builders. Oh yes—and the individuals they empower.

In the contemporary idiom, that's where it's at. So, get with it!

Go build a team!

About the Author

Woodrow H. Sears earned one of the early doctorates in Human Resource Development, studying under Leonard Nadler at George Washington University, the man who coined the term and created the professional academic discipline known as HRD. Before beginning his career in management, Woody was a photographer; a newspaper reporter; a Marine officer; and later an editor with the Cooperative Extension Service at North Carolina University, where he earned a master's degree in adult education. He worked at Leadership Resources Inc., one of the country's first behaviorally-oriented consulting firms, and served as HR manager and later the director of training for an environmental company. He has provided consulting services for a broad range of industries and technologies, U.S. federal agencies, and Canadian crown corporations and provincial governments.

After extensive Civil Rights, EEO, and police training, Woody Sears shifted his focus to project management, developing project-management systems for domestic and international clients and lecturing at universities. The author of *Back in Working Order: How American Enterprises Can Win the Productivity Battle* (Scott Foresman, 1984) and co-author with Audrone Tamulion-nyte-Lentz of *Succeeding in Business in Central and Eastern Europe: A Guide to Cultures, Markets, and Practices* (Butterworth-Heinemann, 2001), Woody was in Slovakia as a volunteer with the International Executive Service Corps in 1998 when he was asked to go to Lithuania for a one-month assignment. He is still there.

Woody Sears can be contacted at the following e-mail address:

Woodysears@yahoo.com